JESUS
OF NAZARETH

JESUS
OF NAZARETH

The Infancy Narratives

Joseph Ratzinger
Pope Benedict XVI

Translated by Philip J. Whitmore

IMAGE

New York

Translation copyright © 2012 by Libreria Editrice Vaticana

Published in the United States by Image,
an imprint of the Crown Publishing Group,
a division of Random House, Inc., New York.
www.crownpublishing.com

Original title: *Jesus von Nazareth. Prolog. Die Kindheitsgeschichten* (German)
© 2012 Libreria Editrice Vaticana, Città del Vaticano
© 2012 RCS Libri S.p.A., Milano

Library of Congress Cataloging-in-Publication Data
is available upon request

ISBN 978-0-385-34640-5
eISBN 978-0-385-3464-12

PRINTED IN THE UNITED STATES OF AMERICA

Book design based on a design by Maria Carella
Jacket design by Jessie Sayward Bright
Jacket illustration: Jesus is shown to the Three Kings. Codex of Predix (1476). Italy.
Photo © Tarker/The Bridgeman Art Library

5   7   9   10   8   6   4

First Edition

CONTENTS

The following abbreviations are used for books of the Bible:

Acts	Acts of the Apostles	Hos	Hosea
		Is	Isaiah
Amos	Amos	Jas	James
Bar	Baruch	Jer	Jeremiah
1 Chron	1 Chronicles	Jn	John
2 Chron	2 Chronicles	1 Jn	1 John
Col	Colossians	2 Jn	2 John
1 Cor	1 Corinthians	3 Jn	3 John
2 Cor	2 Corinthians	Job	Job
Dan	Daniel	Joel	Joel
Deut	Deuteronomy	Jon	Jonah
Eccles	Ecclesiastes	Josh	Joshua
Eph	Ephesians	Jud	Judith
Esther	Esther	Jude	Jude
Ex	Exodus	Judg	Judges
Ezek	Ezekiel	1 Kings	1 Kings
Ezra	Ezra	2 Kings	2 Kings
Gal	Galatians	Lam	Lamentations
Gen	Genesis	Lev	Leviticus
Hab	Habakkuk	Lk	Luke
Hag	Haggai	1 Mac	1 Maccabees
Heb	Hebrews	2 Mac	2 Maccabees

Mal	Malachi	Rom	Romans
Mic	Micah	Ruth	Ruth
Mk	Mark	1 Sam	1 Samuel
Mt	Matthew	2 Sam	2 Samuel
Nahum	Nahum	Sir	Sirach
Neh	Nehemiah		(Ecclesiasticus)
Num	Numbers	Song	Song of Solomon
Obad	Obadiah	1 Thess	1 Thessalonians
1 Pet	1 Peter	2 Thess	2 Thessalonians
2 Pet	2 Peter	1 Tim	1 Timothy
Phil	Philippians	2 Tim	2 Timothy
Philem	Philemon	Tit	Titus
Prov	Proverbs	Tob	Tobit
Ps	Psalms	Wis	Wisdom
Rev	Revelation	Zech	Zechariah
	(Apocalypse)	Zeph	Zephaniah

Publisher's Note

The Revised Standard Version (RSV) is the preferred translation for Scriptural quotations within the text. In some instances, however, in order to reflect as clearly as possible the verbal associations emphasized by the author, it has been necessary to translate directly from the original biblical text.

This short book on Jesus' infancy narratives, which I have been promising to write for some time, is at last ready to be presented to the reader. It is not a third volume, but a kind of small "antechamber" to the two earlier volumes on the figure and the message of Jesus of Nazareth. I have set out here, in dialogue with exegetes past and present, to interpret what Matthew and Luke say about Jesus' infancy at the beginning of their Gospels.

I am convinced that good exegesis involves two stages. Firstly one has to ask what the respective authors intended to convey through their text in their own day—the historical component of exegesis. But it is not sufficient to leave the text in the past and thus relegate it to history. The second question posed by good exegesis must be: is what I read here true? Does it concern me? If so, how? With a text like the Bible, whose ultimate and fundamental author, according to our faith, is God himself, the question regarding the here and now of things past is undeniably included in the task of exegesis. The seriousness of the historical quest is in no way diminished by this: on the contrary, it is enhanced.

In this sense, I have taken pains to enter into dialogue

with the texts. In so doing I have been conscious that this conversation, drawing in the past, the present and the future, can never come to an end, and that every exegesis must fall short of the magnitude of the biblical text. My hope is that this short book, despite its limitations, will be able to help many people on their path toward and alongside Jesus.

Castel Gandolfo, on the Solemnity of the
Assumption of the Blessed Virgin Mary
15 August 2012

Joseph Ratzinger—Benedict XVI

CHAPTER I

"Where Are You From?" (John 19:9)

THE QUESTION ABOUT JESUS' ORIGIN AS A QUESTION ABOUT BEING AND MISSION

While he was interrogating Jesus, Pilate unexpectedly put this question to the accused: "Where are you from?" Jesus' accusers had called for him to receive the death penalty by dramatically declaring that this Jesus had made himself the Son of God—a capital offense under the law. The "enlightened" Roman judge, who had already expressed skepticism regarding the question of truth (cf. *Jn* 18:38), could easily have found this claim by the accused laughable. And yet he was frightened. The accused had indicated that he was a king, but that his kingdom was "not of this world" (*Jn* 18:36). And then he had alluded to a mysterious origin and purpose, saying: "For this I was born and for this I have come into the world, to bear witness to the truth" (*Jn* 18:37).

All this must have seemed like madness to the Roman

judge. And yet he could not shake off the mysterious impression left by this man, so different from those he had met before who resisted Roman domination and fought for the restoration of the kingdom of Israel. The Roman judge asks where Jesus is from in order to understand who he really is and what he wants.

The question about Jesus' provenance, as an inquiry after his deeper origin and hence his true being, is also found in other key passages of Saint John's Gospel, and it plays an equally important role in the Synoptic Gospels. For John, as for the Synoptics, it raises a singular paradox. On the one hand, counting against Jesus and his claim to a divine mission, is the fact that people knew exactly where he was from: he does not come from heaven, from "the Father," from "above," as he purports to (*Jn* 8:23). No: "Is not this Jesus, whose father and mother we know? How does he now say, 'I have come down from heaven'?" (*Jn* 6:42).

The Synoptics tell of a similar dispute that arose in the synagogue at Nazareth, Jesus' hometown. Jesus had expounded the words of sacred Scripture not in the customary manner, but by relating them to himself and his mission with an authority that went beyond the bounds of all exegesis (cf. *Lk* 4:21). The listeners were understandably shocked by this treatment of Scripture, by the claim that he himself was the inner point of reference and the key to exegesis of the sacred text. Shock led to denial: "'Is not this the carpenter, the son of Mary and brother of James and Joses and Judas and Simon, and are not his sisters here with us?' And they took offense at him" (*Mk* 6:3).

They know perfectly well who Jesus is and where he comes from—he is one among others. He is one like us. His claim can only be presumption. Moreover, Nazareth was not associated with any such promise. John recounts that Philip said to Nathanael: "We have found him of whom Moses in the law and also the prophets wrote: Jesus of Nazareth, the son of Joseph." Nathanael's response is well known: "Can anything good come out of Nazareth?" (*Jn* 1:45f.). The ordinariness of Jesus, the provincial carpenter, seems not to conceal a mystery of any kind. His origin marks him out as one like any other.

Yet the reverse argument is also adduced against Jesus' authority, as in the dispute with the man born blind, after he received his sight: "We know that God has spoken to Moses, but as for this man [Jesus], we do not know where he comes from" (*Jn* 9:29).

When Jesus preached in their synagogue, the people of Nazareth had said something rather similar, before dismissing him as someone well-known to them and just like them: "Where did this man get all this? What is the wisdom given to him? What mighty works are wrought by his hands!"

(*Mk* 6:2). Here too the question "where is he from?" arises—only to be dismissed straight away by the reference to his relatives.

Jesus' provenance is both known and unknown, seemingly easy to establish, and yet not exhaustively. In Caesarea Philippi, Jesus will ask his disciples: "Who do people say that I am? . . . Who do you say that I am?" (*Mk* 8:27ff.). Who is Jesus? Where is he from? The two questions are inseparably linked.

The four Gospels set out to answer these questions. They were written in order to supply an answer. Matthew opens his Gospel with Jesus' genealogy because he wants to put the question of Jesus' provenance in the correct light from the very beginning: the genealogy serves as a kind of heading to the entire Gospel. Luke, on the other hand, places Jesus' genealogy at the beginning of his public ministry, as a kind of public presentation of Jesus, in order to answer the same question with a different emphasis—in anticipation of all that is about to unfold in the rest of the Gospel. Let us now try to understand more closely the essential purpose of the two genealogies.

For Matthew, two names are of key significance if we are to understand Jesus' provenance: Abraham and David.

The story of the promise begins with Abraham, following the dispersal of mankind after the building of the Tower of Babel. Abraham points ahead to what is yet to come. He is a wayfarer, not only from the land of his birth into the promised land, but also on the journey from the present into the future. His whole life points forward, it is a dynamic of walking along the path of what is to come. Thus the Letter to the Hebrews rightly presents him as a pilgrim of faith on the basis of the promise: "He looked forward to the city which has foundations, whose builder and maker is God" (11:10). For Abraham, the promise refers in the first instance to his descendants, but it also extends further: "all the nations of the earth shall bless themselves by him" (*Gen* 18:18). Thus the whole history, beginning with Abraham and leading to Jesus, is open toward universality—through Abraham, blessing comes to all.

From the beginning of the genealogy, then, the focus is already on the end of the Gospel, when the risen Lord says to the disciples: "Make disciples of all nations" (*Mt* 28:19). In the particular history revealed by the genealogy, this movement toward the whole is present from the beginning: the universality of Jesus' mission is already contained within his origin.

Both the genealogy and the history that it recounts are largely structured around the figure of David, the king to whom the promise of an eternal kingdom had been given: "Your throne shall be established for ever" (2 *Sam* 7:16). The genealogy that Matthew puts before us is steeped in this promise. It is constructed in three sets of fourteen generations, at first rising from Abraham to David, then descending from Solomon to the Babylonian captivity, and then rising again to Jesus, in whom the promise comes to fulfillment. The king who is to last for ever now appears—looking quite different, though, from what the Davidic model might have led one to expect.

This threefold division becomes even clearer if we bear in mind that the Hebrew letters of the name "David" add up to fourteen: even in terms of number symbolism, then, the path from Abraham to Jesus bears the clear imprint of David, his name and his promise. On this basis one could say that the genealogy, with its three sets of fourteen generations, is truly a Gospel of Christ the King: the whole of history looks toward him whose throne is to endure for ever.

Matthew's genealogy traces the male line, but in the course of it, prior to Mary who appears at the end, four women are mentioned by name: Tamar, Rahab, Ruth and the wife of Uriah. Why do these women appear in the genealogy? By what criterion are they chosen?

It has been said that all four women were sinners. So their inclusion here would serve to indicate that Jesus took upon himself their sins—and with them the sins of the world—and that his mission was the justification of sinners.

But this cannot have been the determining factor for the selection, not least because it does not in fact apply to all four women. More important, none of these women were Jewish. So through them the world of the Gentiles enters the genealogy of Jesus—his mission to Jews *and* Gentiles is made manifest.

Yet most important of all is the fact that the genealogy ends with a woman: Mary, who truly marks a new beginning and relativizes the entire genealogy. Throughout the generations, we find the formula: "Abraham was the father of Isaac . . ." But at the end, there is something quite different. In Jesus' case there is no reference to fatherhood, instead we read: "Jacob [was] the father of Joseph the husband of Mary, of whom Jesus was born, who is called Christ" (*Mt* 1:16). In the account of Jesus' birth that follows immediately afterward, Matthew tells us that Joseph was not Jesus' father and that he wanted to dismiss Mary on account of her supposed adultery. But this is what is said to him: "That which is conceived in Mary is of the Holy Spirit" (*Mt* 1:20). So the final sentence turns the whole genealogy around. Mary is a new beginning. Her child does not originate from any man, but is a new creation, conceived through the Holy Spirit.

The genealogy is still important: Joseph is the legal father of Jesus. Through him, Jesus belongs by law, "legally," to the house of David. And yet he comes from elsewhere, "from above"—from God himself. The mystery of his provenance, his dual origin, confronts us quite concretely: his origin can be named and yet it is a mystery. Only God is truly his "father." The human genealogy has a certain significance in terms of world history. And yet in the end it is Mary, the lowly virgin from Nazareth, in whom a new beginning takes place, in whom human existence starts afresh.

Let us take a look now at the genealogy found in Luke's Gospel (cf. 3:23–38). Several differences strike us vis-à-vis the list of ancestors supplied by Saint Matthew.

We have already established that this genealogy introduces the public ministry, it so to speak legitimizes Jesus in his public mission, whereas Matthew presents the genealogy as the very start of the Gospel, proceeding from there to the account of Jesus' conception and birth, and thus unfolding the question of his provenance in its dual significance.

A further striking difference is that Matthew and Luke agree on only a handful of names; not even the name of Joseph's father is common to the two. How can this be? Apart from elements drawn from the Old Testament, both authors have based themselves on traditions whose sources we cannot reconstruct. It seems to me utterly futile to formulate hypotheses on this matter. Neither evangelist is concerned so much with the individual names as with the symbolic structure within which Jesus' place in history is set before us: the intricacy with which he is woven into the historical strands of the promise, as well as the *new beginning* which paradoxically characterizes his origin side by side with the *continuity* of God's action in history.

A further difference consists in the fact that whereas Matthew climbs from the beginnings—from the root—to the present, to the top of the "tree," Luke on the contrary descends from Jesus, the "treetop," down to the roots, in order to show that in the end the ultimate root is found not in the depths but rather in the "heights"—God is there at the beginning of human existence: "Enos, the son of Seth, the son of Adam, the son of God" (*Lk* 3:38).

An element common to Matthew and Luke is that the genealogy breaks off and comes to a stop when it reaches Joseph: "Jesus, when he began his ministry, was about thirty years of age, being the son (as was supposed) of Joseph" (*Lk* 3:23). Legally he was considered Joseph's son, as Luke tells us. Yet Jesus' true origin had already been made clear in the first two chapters of Luke's Gospel.

Whereas Matthew gives a clear and theologically symbolic structure to his genealogy, with its three sets of fourteen names, Luke arranges his 76 names without any outwardly recognizable pattern. Yet here too a symbolic structuring of historical time can be detected: the genealogy contains eleven times seven members. Luke may have known the apocalyptic formula that divides world history into twelve parts and at the end consists of eleven times seven generations. So this could be a discreet way of indicating that with Jesus "the fullness of time" had come, that with him the decisive hour of world history had dawned: he is the new Adam, who once again comes "from God"—but in a more radical way than the first Adam, not merely breathed into being by God, but truly God's "Son." While for Matthew it is the Davidic promise that permeates the symbolic structuring of time, Luke, in tracing the line back to Adam, wants to show that humanity starts afresh in Jesus. The genealogy expresses a promise that concerns the whole of humanity.

In this connection, another reading of Luke's genealogy is worth mentioning, one that we find in the writings of Saint Irenaeus. The text he was using had not 76 but 72 names. 72 (or 70) was the number, derived from *Ex* 1:5, that indicated the number of people in the world—a figure that appears in the Lucan tradition of 72 (or 70) disciples, whom Jesus set alongside the twelve Apostles. Irenaeus writes as follows: "To prove this, Luke shows that the genealogy of our Lord, which extends to Adam, contains seventy-two generations, and so he joins the end to the beginning and points out that it is he [Christ] who recapitulates in himself all the nations that had been dispersed from Adam onward, and all the tongues, and the human race, including Adam himself. Hence Paul, too, styled Adam a type of the one who was to come" (*Adv. Haer.* III, 22,3).

Even if the authentic Lucan text does not contain at this point the symbolism of the 70, on which Saint Irenaeus' exegesis depends, nevertheless the underlying intention of Luke's genealogy is correctly grasped here. Jesus takes upon himself the whole of humanity, the whole history of man, and he gives it a decisive re-orientation toward a new manner of human existence.

John the evangelist, who repeatedly raises the question of Jesus' provenance, does not present a genealogy at the beginning of his Gospel, but in the Prologue he grandly and emphatically proposes an answer to that question. At the same time he expands his answer to the question into a definition of Christian life: on the basis of Jesus' provenance he sheds light upon the identity of his followers.

"In the beginning was the Word, and the Word was with God, and the Word was God . . . and the Word became flesh and dwelt [pitched his tent] among us" (*Jn* 1:1–14). The man Jesus is the dwelling-place of the Word, the eternal divine Word, in this world. Jesus' "flesh," his human existence, is the "dwelling" or "tent" of the Word: the reference to the sacred tent of Israel in the wilderness is unmistakable. Jesus is, so to speak, the tent of meeting—he is the reality for which the tent and the later Temple could only serve as signs. Jesus' origin, his provenance, is the true "beginning"—the primordial source from which all things come, the "light" that makes the world into the cosmos. He comes from God. He is God. This "beginning" that has come to us opens up—as a beginning—a new manner of human existence. "For to all who received him, who believed in his name, he gave power to become children of God; who were born, not of blood nor of the will of the flesh nor of the will of man, but of God" (*Jn* 1:12f.).

One version of the manuscript tradition preserves a reading of this sentence not in the plural but in the singular: "who was born, not of blood . . ." This makes the sentence into a clear reference to the virginal conception and birth of Jesus. Jesus' being from God, as affirmed by the tradition preserved by Matthew and Luke, would be concretely underlined once more. But this is only a secondary reading: the authentic text of the Gospel speaks quite clearly here of those who believe in Christ's name and who receive a new origin through that name. Yet the connection with the confession of Jesus' birth from the Virgin Mary is undeniably present: those who believe in Jesus enter through faith into Jesus' unique new origin, and they receive this origin as their own. In and of themselves, all these believers are initially "born of blood and of the will of man." But their faith gives them a new birth: they enter into the origin of Jesus Christ, which now becomes their own origin. From Christ, through faith in him, they are now born of God.

So John has recapitulated the deepest meaning of the genealogies, and moreover he has taught us to understand them as an interpretation of our own origin, our true "genealogy." Just as the genealogies break off at the end, because

Jesus was not begotten by Joseph, but was truly born of the Holy Spirit from the Virgin Mary, so it can now be said of us that our true "genealogy" is faith in Jesus, who gives us a new origin, who brings us to birth "from God."

The Annunciation of the Birth of John the Baptist and the Annunciation of the Birth of Jesus

On the particular literary character of the texts

All four Gospels place the figure of John the Baptist at the beginning of Jesus' ministry and they reveal him as the one who prepared the way for Jesus. Saint Luke presents the connection between the two figures and their respective missions at an earlier stage, in a shared infancy narrative. Even in conception and birth, Jesus and John are linked together.

Before we consider the content of the texts, a brief word about their particular literary character is necessary. In their different ways, both Matthew and Luke closely link the events of Jesus' childhood with Old Testament passages.

Matthew demonstrates the connections for the reader each time by quoting the corresponding Old Testament text. Luke describes events using Old Testament language—making allusions that in individual cases could often seem coincidental and cannot always be proven, yet their overall effect on the fabric of the texts is unmistakable.

In Luke, there seems to be an underlying Hebrew text; at any rate, the whole account is marked by Semitisms, which are not otherwise typical of Luke. Attempts have been made to explain the particular character of these two chapters (*Lk* 1–2) in terms of a literary genre found in early Judaism: a Haggadic Midrash, that is to say, an exegesis of Scripture by means of narratives. The literary resemblance is beyond dispute. And yet it is clear that Luke's infancy narrative is not a product of early Judaism, but belongs firmly to early Christianity.

There is more. A story is told here which interprets the Scriptures. And the converse is also true: what the Scriptures intended to say in many passages becomes visible only now through this new story. It is a story that is completely rooted in the word and yet only now does it supply the full meaning of that word, which hitherto could not be recognized. The story told here is no mere illustration of the ancient words: it is the reality to which they were referring. In those words alone it could not be recognized, but they now attain their full meaning through the event in which they come to pass.

. . .

If that is so, the question arises: how did Matthew and Luke come to know the story that they recount? What are their sources? As Joachim Gnilka rightly says, it is evidently a matter of family traditions. Luke indicates from time to time that Mary, the Mother of Jesus, is herself one of his sources, especially when he says in 2:51 that "his mother kept all these things in her heart" (cf. also 2:19). Only she could report the event of the annunciation, for which there were no human witnesses.

Naturally, modern "critical" exegesis will tend to dismiss such connections as naive. But why should there not have been a tradition of this kind, preserved in the most intimate circle and theologically elaborated at the same time? Why should Luke have invented the statement about Mary keeping the words and events in her heart, if there were no concrete grounds for saying so? Why should he have spoken of her "pondering" over the words (*Lk* 2:19; cf. 1:29) if nothing was known of this?

I would add that the late emergence, particularly of the Marian traditions, can be similarly explained by the discretion of the Lord's mother and of those around her: the sacred events of her early life could not be made public while she was still alive.

. . .

To sum up: what Matthew and Luke set out to do, each in his own way, was not to tell "stories" but to write history, real history that had actually happened, admittedly interpreted and understood in the context of the word of God. Hence the aim was not to produce an exhaustive account, but a record of what seemed important for the nascent faith community in the light of the word. The infancy narratives are interpreted history, condensed and written down in accordance with the interpretation.

There is a reciprocal relationship between the interpreting word of God and the interpreting history: the word of God teaches that "salvation history," universal in scope, is present within the events. For their part, the events themselves unlock the word of God and manifest the true reality hidden within the individual texts.

The Old Testament contains some passages that are still, as it were, "stray." Marius Reiser cites *Is* 53 as an example. One could relate the text to this or that figure, perhaps to Jeremiah. But the actual "owner" of the text keeps us waiting. Only when he appears does the passage acquire its full meaning. The same applies, as we shall see, to *Is* 7:14. This is another of the passages that, at the time of writing, were still waiting for the figure to whom they refer.

One of the characteristics of early Christian narrative is that it provides these "waiting" words with their "owner." This connection between the "waiting" word and the recognition of its "owner," now that he has appeared, has given rise to the typically Christian approach to exegesis, which is new and yet remains utterly faithful to the original words of Scripture.

THE ANNUNCIATION OF THE BIRTH OF JOHN

After these preliminary considerations, we now turn to the texts themselves. In the first instance, we are dealing here with two groups of narratives, different in character and yet quite closely related: the birth and childhood of John the Baptist and the annunciation that Mary would give birth to Jesus the Messiah.

The story of John has particularly deep Old Testament roots. Zechariah is a priest from the division of Abijah. His wife Elizabeth is also of priestly stock: she is from the tribe of Aaron (cf. *Lk* 1:5). According to Old Testament law, the service of priests is tied to membership of the tribe of the sons of Aaron and Levi. So John the Baptist is a priest. In him the priesthood of the Old Covenant moves toward Jesus; it becomes a pointer toward Jesus, a proclamation of his mission.

It strikes me as important that in John the whole Old Covenant priesthood becomes a prophecy of Jesus, and so— together with Psalm 118, the highest expression of its theology and spirituality—it points toward him, it makes itself his. A one-sided emphasis on the contrast between the Old

Testament sacrificial cult and the spiritual worship of the New Covenant (cf. *Rom* 12:1) would obscure this connecting line, this inner dynamic of the Old Testament priesthood, which is a path toward Jesus Christ not only in John but earlier too, in the development of priestly spirituality expressed in Psalm 118.

The characterization of Zechariah and Elizabeth found in the following verse of Luke's Gospel (1:6) likewise points toward the inner unity of the two testaments. It is said of both spouses that they were righteous before God, and that they walked blamelessly in all the commandments and precepts of the Lord. When we come to consider the figure of Saint Joseph we will look more closely at the term "righteous" or "just," in which the whole piety of the Old Covenant is summed up. The "just" are those who inwardly live the ordinances of the law aright—those who walk their path in righteousness, according to the revealed will of God and open up space for new action by the Lord. In them, Old and New Covenant converge and combine to form a single history of God with men.

Zechariah enters the Temple; he enters the sacred space, while the people wait outside and pray. It is the hour of the evening sacrifice when he places incense on the burning coals. The fragrance of the rising incense is a symbol of prayer: "Let my prayer be counted as incense before you, and the lifting up of my hands as an evening sacrifice," as we read in *Ps* 141:2. The Book of Revelation describes the heavenly liturgy in these terms: the four living creatures and the twenty-four elders were each "holding a harp, and . . . golden bowls full of incense, which are the prayers of the saints" (5:8). At this hour, in which heavenly and earthly liturgies unite, there appears to the priest Zechariah "an angel of the Lord," whose name is not yet indicated. He stands "on the right side of the altar of incense" (*Lk* 1:11). Erik Peterson describes the positioning as follows: "This was the south side of the altar. The angel stands between the altar and the seven-branched candlestick. On the left, the north side of the altar, stood the table with the bread-offerings" (*Lukasevangelium*, p. 22).

Place and time are holy: this new step in salvation history is in complete harmony with the ordinances of the divine Covenant of Sinai. In the Temple itself, during its liturgy, the new begins: the inner continuity of God's dealings with men is very powerfully manifested. This corresponds to the ending of Saint Luke's Gospel: as the Lord is about to ascend into heaven, he tells the disciples to return to Jerusalem, *there* to receive the gift of the Holy Spirit and *from there* to bring the Gospel to the world (cf. *Lk* 24:49–53).

At the same time, we must note the difference between the annunciation of the birth of the Baptist to Zechariah and the annunciation of the birth of Jesus to Mary. Zechariah, father of the Baptist, is a priest and he receives the message in the Temple, during its liturgy. Mary's lineage is not mentioned. The angel Gabriel is sent to her by God. He enters her house in Nazareth—a town unknown to the sacred Scriptures, a house that we must surely picture to ourselves as very humble and very simple. The contrast between the two scenes could not be greater: priest—Temple—liturgy on the one hand, an unknown young woman—an unknown small town—an unknown private dwelling on the other. The sign of the new Covenant is humility, hiddenness—the sign of the mustard-seed. The Son of God comes in lowliness. Both these elements belong together: the profound continuity in the history of God's action and the radical newness of the hidden mustard-seed.

Let us return to Zechariah and the annunciation of the message of John the Baptist's birth. It is not only the location that gives the promise an Old Covenant flavor. Everything said here, everything that happens here, is saturated in the words of sacred Scripture in the manner described above. It is only through these new events that the words acquire their full meaning—and vice versa: the events are of enduring significance because they proceed from the word, they are "fulfilled word." Two groups of Old Testament texts come together here to form a new unity.

First of all, there is a group of stories about infertile parents receiving the promise of a son, who thus appears as a gift from God himself. The prime example is the annunciation of the birth of Isaac, heir to the promise that God had made to Abraham: "The Lord said, 'I will surely return to you in the spring, and Sarah your wife shall have a son' . . . Abraham and Sarah were old, advanced in age; it had ceased to be with Sarah after the manner of women. So Sarah laughed to herself . . . The Lord said to Abraham, 'Why did Sarah laugh? . . . Is anything too hard for the Lord?'" (*Gen* 18:10–14). Closely related to this is the story of the birth of Samuel. His mother Hannah was barren. On hearing her impassioned prayer, the priest Eli promised that God would grant her request. She became pregnant and consecrated her son Samuel to the Lord (cf. 1 *Sam* 1). So John belongs to a long line of offspring born to infertile parents through a miraculous intervention of God, for whom nothing is impossible. Because he comes from God in this special way, he belongs completely to God, and hence he also lives completely for men, in order to lead them to God.

When it is said of John that he "shall drink no wine nor strong drink" (*Lk* 1:15), this likewise aligns him within the priestly tradition. "Concerning the priests who are consecrated to God, it is said: 'Drink no wine nor strong drink, you nor your sons with you, when you go into the tent of meeting, lest you die; it shall be a statute for ever throughout your generations' (*Lev* 10:9)" (Stöger, *Das Evangelium nach Lukas*, p. 31). John, who will be filled with the Holy Spirit from his mother's womb (cf. *Lk* 1:15), lives permanently, as it were, "in the tent of meeting": he is a priest not only at certain moments, but with his whole existence, and in this way he proclaims the new priesthood that will appear with Jesus.

In addition to this group of texts, which come from the historical books of the Old Testament, there are prophetic texts from the Books of Malachi and Daniel that shape the dialogue between the angel and Zechariah.

Let us hear Malachi first: "Behold, I will send you Elijah the prophet before the great and terrible day of the Lord comes. And he will turn the hearts of fathers to their children and the hearts of children to their fathers" (3:23f.). "Behold, I send my messenger to prepare the way before me, and the Lord whom you seek will suddenly come to his temple; the messenger of the covenant in whom you delight, behold, he is coming, says the Lord of hosts" (3:1). John's mission is interpreted in terms of the figure of Elijah. He is not to be identified with Elijah, but he comes in the spirit and power of the great prophet. To this extent, he does indeed fulfill through his mission the expectation that Elijah would return to purify the people of God and put it back on its feet, thus preparing it for the arrival of the Lord himself. So on the one hand John is placed in the category of the prophets, and yet at the same time he is raised above them, inasmuch as the returning Elijah prepares the way for the coming of God himself. So in these texts, the figure of Jesus and the coming of Jesus is tacitly identified with the coming of God himself.

In Jesus it is the Lord who comes, in this way giving history its definitive direction.

The prophet Daniel is the second prophetic voice present in the background of our story. The Book of Daniel is the only one that mentions Gabriel by name. This great divine messenger appears to the prophet "at the time of the evening sacrifice" (9:21), to communicate a message about the future destiny of the chosen people. In response to Zechariah's doubts, the divine messenger reveals himself as "Gabriel, who stands in the presence of God" (*Lk* 1:19).

In the Book of Daniel, the revelations communicated by Gabriel include the mysterious numerical indications about imminent hardships and the timing of the definitive salvation which it is the archangel's principal task to announce, amid all the tribulations. Both Jewish and Christian thinkers have repeatedly grappled with these coded figures. Particular attention has been focused on the prophecy of the seventy weeks which "are decreed concerning your people and your holy city . . . to bring in everlasting righteousness" (9:24). René Laurentin has tried to show that Luke's infancy narrative follows a precise chronology, according to which from the moment of the annunciation to Zechariah until the presentation of Jesus in the Temple, 490 days elapsed, that is to say seventy weeks of seven days each (cf. *Structure et*

Théologie, pp. 49ff.). Whether Luke consciously adopted this chronology must remain an open question.

Be that as it may, in the account of the apparition of the archangel Gabriel at the hour of the evening sacrifice, we can surely see a reference to Daniel, a reference to the promise of everlasting righteousness entering time. In this way, the evangelist is saying to us: the time is fulfilled. The hidden event that takes place during Zechariah's evening sacrifice, unnoticed by the vast world public, in reality ushers in the eschatological hour—the hour of salvation.

THE ANNUNCIATION TO MARY

"In the sixth month the angel Gabriel was sent from God to a city of Galilee named Nazareth, to a virgin betrothed to a man whose name was Joseph, of the house of David; and the virgin's name was Mary" (*Lk* 1:26f.). In the first place, the annunciation of the birth of Jesus is linked chronologically with the story of John the Baptist by the reference to the time that has elapsed since the archangel Gabriel's message to Zechariah, that is to say "in the sixth month" of Elizabeth's pregnancy. The two events and the two missions are also linked in this passage by the indication that Mary and Elizabeth, and hence their offspring too, are blood relatives.

Mary's visit to Elizabeth, made as a consequence of the

dialogue between Gabriel and Mary (cf. *Lk* 1:36), occasions an encounter in the Holy Spirit between Jesus and John even before they are born, and this encounter at the same time makes visible the relationship between their respective missions: Jesus is the younger of the two, the one who comes later. But he is the one whose proximity causes John to leap in his mother's womb and fills Elizabeth with the Holy Spirit (cf. *Lk* 1:41). So in Luke's annunciation and nativity narratives, what the Baptist was to say in John's Gospel is already objectively present: "This is he of whom I said, 'After me comes a man who ranks before me, for he was before me'" (1:30).

Now, though, it is time to look more closely at the story of the annunciation to Mary of the birth of Jesus. First let us consider the angel's message, then Mary's answer.

A striking feature of the angel's greeting is that he does not address Mary with the usual Hebrew salutation *shalom*—peace be with you—but with the Greek greeting formula *chaīre*, which we might well translate with the word "Hail," as in the Church's Marian prayer, pieced together from the words of the annunciation narrative (cf. *Lk* 1:28, 42). Yet at this point it is only right to draw out the true meaning of the word *chaīre*: rejoice! This exclamation from the angel—we could say—marks the true beginning of the New Testament.

The word reappears during the Holy Night on the lips

of the angel who says to the shepherds: "I bring you good news of a great joy" (*Lk* 2:10). It appears again—in John's Gospel—at the encounter with the risen Lord: "The disciples were glad when they saw the Lord" (20:20). Jesus' farewell discourses in Saint John's Gospel present a theology of joy, which as it were illuminates the depth of this word. "I will see you again and your hearts will rejoice, and no one will take your joy from you" (16:22).

Joy appears in these texts as the particular gift of the Holy Spirit, the true gift of the Redeemer. So a chord is sounded with the angel's salutation which then resounds throughout the life of the Church. Its content is also present in the fundamental word that serves to designate the entire Christian message: *Gospel—good news.*

"Rejoice"—as we have seen—is in the first instance a Greek greeting, and to that extent this pronouncement by the angel immediately opens the door to the peoples of the world: the universality of the Christian message becomes evident. And yet this word is also taken from the Old Testament, and thus it expresses the complete continuity of biblical salvation history. Stanislas Lyonnet and René Laurentin in particular have shown that Gabriel's greeting to Mary takes up and brings into the present the prophecy of *Zeph* 3:14–17: "Rejoice, daughter of Zion; shout, Israel . . . the King of Israel, the Lord, is in your midst."

There is no need here to enter into a detailed textual comparison between the angel's greeting to Mary and Zephaniah's prophecy. The essential reason for the daughter of Zion to rejoice is stated in the text itself: "the Lord is in your midst" (*Zeph* 3:15,17). Literally it says: "he is in your womb." Here Zephaniah is alluding to a passage in the Book of Exodus which speaks of God dwelling in the ark of the Covenant as dwelling "in Israel's womb" (cf. Laurentin, *Structure et Théologie,* pp. 70f., with reference to *Ex* 33:3 and 34:9). This same word reappears in Gabriel's message to Mary: "you will conceive in your womb" (*Lk* 1:31).

Whatever view is taken regarding the details of these parallels, there is clearly an inner resemblance between the two messages. Mary appears as the daughter of Zion in person. The Zion prophecies are fulfilled in her in an unexpected way. Mary becomes the Ark of the Covenant, the place where the Lord truly dwells.

"Rejoice, full of grace!" One further aspect of the greeting *chaîre* is worthy of note: the connection between joy and grace. In Greek, the two words joy and grace (*chará* and *cháris*) are derived from the same root. Joy and grace belong together.

Let us turn now to the content of the promise. Mary is to bear a child, to whom the angel assigns the titles "Son of the Most High" and "Son of God." Moreover, it is promised that God, the Lord, will give him the throne of his father

David. He will rule over the house of Jacob for ever, and his kingdom (his reign) will have no end. Then comes a series of promises, which reveal how the conception is to take place. "The Holy Spirit will come upon you, and the power of the Most High will overshadow you; therefore the child to be born will be called holy, the Son of God" (*Lk* 1:35).

Let us begin with this final element. In terms of the language used, it belongs to the theology of the Temple and of God's presence in the sanctuary. The sacred cloud—the *shekinah*—is the visible sign of God's presence. It conceals the fact that God is dwelling in his house, yet at the same time points to it. The cloud that casts its shadow over men comes back later in the account of the Lord's transfiguration (cf. *Lk* 9:34; *Mk* 9:7). Again it is a sign of God's presence, of God's self-revelation in hiddenness. So the reference to the overshadowing by the Holy Spirit brings us back to the Zion theology of the salutation. Once again Mary appears as God's living tent, in which he chooses to dwell among men in a new way.

At the same time, the mystery of the Triune God is evoked in the course of this annunciation message. It is God the Father who acts, promising that David's throne will endure and now appointing the heir whose kingdom will have no end—David's definitive heir, whom the prophet Nathan had foretold with the words: "I will be his father, and he shall be my son" (2 *Sam* 7:14). Psalm 2 takes up the same idea: "You are my son, today I have begotten you" (v. 7).

The angel's words remain entirely within the realm of

Old Testament piety, and yet they transcend it. In the light of this new situation, they take on a new realism, a hitherto unforeseeable depth and strength. At this stage, the Trinitarian mystery has not yet been thought through, it has not been worked into a definitive teaching. It appears spontaneously in and through God's way of acting, as prefigured in the Old Testament; it appears within the event, without at this stage becoming a doctrine. Similarly, the sonship of the child is not thought through in metaphysical terms. Everything remains within the realm of Jewish piety. Yet the ancient words take on a new life; they transcend themselves on account of the new event that they express and interpret. In their very simplicity, they acquire an almost disturbing new loftiness, which can develop further only in the path of Jesus and in the path of the believer.

In this context, too, we encounter the name "Jesus," which the angel assigns to the promised child both in Luke (1:31) and in Matthew (1:21). Concealed within the name of Jesus is the tetragrammaton, the mysterious name from Mount Horeb, here expanded into the statement: God saves. The, as it were, "incomplete" name from Sinai is finally spoken. The God who *is*, is the saving God, now present. The revelation of God's name, which began in the burning bush, comes to completion in Jesus (cf. *Jn* 17:26).

. . .

The redemption brought by the promised child would be manifested in the definitive establishment of David's kingship. Permanence had indeed been promised to the Davidic kingdom: "Your house and your kingdom shall be made sure for ever before me; your throne shall be established for ever" (2 Sam 7:16), as Nathan had proclaimed at God's own behest.

Psalm 89 reflects in a disturbing way the contradiction between the definitive nature of the promise and the historical reality of the collapse of David's kingship: "I will establish his line for ever, and his throne as the days of the heavens. If his children forsake my law . . . then I will punish their transgression with the rod . . . but I will not remove from him my steadfast love, or be false to my faithfulness" (vv. 30–34). With these words the psalmist movingly and **insistently repeats that promise back to God, he knocks at** God's heart and implores his faithfulness. For the reality he now experiences is quite different: "but now you have cast off and rejected, you are full of wrath against your anointed, you have renounced the covenant with your servant, you have defiled his crown in the dust . . . all that pass by despoil him, he has become the scorn of his neighbours . . . remember, O Lord, how your servant is scorned!" (vv. 39–42, 51).

This lament by Israel was also present to God at the moment when Gabriel was announcing to the Virgin Mary the new king who would sit on David's throne. Herod was king by favor of Rome. He was an Idumaean, not a son of

David. But more than anything else it was his appalling cruelty that made him such a caricature of the kingship that had been promised to David. The angel announces that God has not forgotten his promise; that it is to come true *now* in the child that Mary will conceive through the Holy Spirit. "His kingdom will have no end," says Gabriel to Mary.

In the fourth century this phrase was incorporated into the Nicene Creed—at a time when the kingship of Jesus of Nazareth already spanned the entire Mediterranean region. We Christians know and gratefully acknowledge that God did indeed carry out his promise. The kingship of Jesus, Son of David, stretches "from sea to sea," from continent to continent, from one century to another.

Admittedly, Jesus' words to Pilate also remain perennially true: "My kingship is not of this world" (*Jn* 18:36). In the course of history, the mighty of this world have sometimes tried to align it with their own, and that is when it is put at risk: they seek to link their power with Jesus' power, and in the process they disfigure his kingdom and endanger it. Or else it is subjected to constant persecution by rulers who will tolerate no other kingdom than their own, and would like to destroy this powerless king, whose mysterious power they still fear.

Yet "his kingdom will have no end": this unique kingdom is not built on worldly power, but is founded on faith and love alone. It is the great force of hope in the midst of a world that so often seems abandoned by God. The kingdom of Jesus, Son of David, knows no end because in him God himself is reigning, in him God's kingdom erupts into this world. The promise that Gabriel spoke to the Virgin Mary is true. It is fulfilled ever anew.

Mary's response, which we will consider now, unfolds in three steps. To begin with, in reaction to the angel's greeting she is troubled and pensive. Her reaction is different from Zechariah's. Of him it is said that he was troubled and "fear fell upon him" (*Lk* 1:12). In Mary's case the first word is the same (she was troubled), but what follows is not fear but an interior reflection on the angel's greeting. She ponders (dialogues within herself) over what the greeting of God's messenger could mean. So one salient feature of the image of the mother of Jesus is already present here, and we will encounter it again in two similar situations in the Gospel: her inner engagement with the word (cf. *Lk* 2:19, 51).

She does not remain locked in her initial troubled state at the proximity of God in his angel, but she seeks to understand. So Mary appears as a fearless woman, one who remains composed even in the presence of something utterly unprecedented. At the same time she stands before us as a woman of great interiority, who holds heart and mind in harmony and seeks to understand the context, the overall significance of God's message. In this way, she becomes an image of the Church as she considers the word of God, tries to understand it in its entirety and guards in her memory the things that have been given to her.

Mary's second reaction is somewhat puzzling for us. After the thoughtful reflection with which she had received his initial greeting, the angel informs her that she has been chosen to be the mother of the Messiah. Mary replies with a short, incisive question: "How shall this be, since I have no husband?" (*Lk* 1:34).

Let us consider again the difference between this response and the reaction of Zechariah, who doubted the possibility of the task announced to him. Like Elizabeth, he was advanced in years: he could no longer hope for a son. Mary, on the other hand, does not doubt. She asks not whether, but how the promise is to be fulfilled, as she cannot recognize any way it could happen: "How shall this be, since I have no husband?" (*Lk* 1:34). This question seems unintelligible to us, because Mary was betrothed, which meant that, according to Jewish law, she was already effectively a married woman, even if she did not yet live with her husband and they had not yet begun their conjugal life.

Since Saint Augustine, one explanation that has been put forward is that Mary had taken a vow of virginity and had entered into the betrothal simply in order to have a protector for her virginity. But this theory is quite foreign to the world of the Judaism of Jesus' time, and in that context it seems inconceivable. So how are we to understand the passage? A satisfying answer has yet to be found by modern exegesis. Some say that at this point, having not yet been taken into the marital home, Mary had had no dealings with men, yet she saw the task as immediately pressing. But this fails to convince, as the time when she would be taken into the marital home could not have been far off. Other exegetes have wanted to view the saying as a purely literary construction, designed to continue the dialogue between Mary and the angel. Yet this is no real explanation of the saying either. Another element to keep in mind is that according to Jewish custom, betrothal was unilaterally pronounced by the man, and the woman was not invited to express her consent. Yet this does not solve the problem either.

So the riddle remains—or perhaps one should say the mystery—of this saying. Mary sees no way, for reasons that are beyond our grasp, that she could become mother of the Messiah through marital relations. The angel confirms that her motherhood will not come about in the normal way after she has been taken home by Joseph, but through "overshadowing, by the power of the Most High," by the coming of the Holy Spirit, and he notes emphatically: "For with God nothing will be impossible" (*Lk* 1:37).

. . .

Next comes the third reaction, Mary's actual answer: her straightforward yes. She declares herself to be the handmaid of the Lord. "Let it be to me according to your word" (*Lk* 1:38).

In one of his Advent homilies, Bernard of Clairvaux offers a stirring presentation of the drama of this moment. After the error of our first parents, the whole world was shrouded in darkness, under the dominion of death. Now God seeks to enter the world anew. He knocks at Mary's door. He needs human freedom. The only way he can redeem man, who was created free, is by means of a free "yes" to his will. In creating freedom, he made himself in a certain sense dependent upon man. His power is tied to the unenforceable "yes" of a human being. So Bernard portrays heaven and earth as it were holding its breath at this moment of the question addressed to Mary. Will she say yes? She hesitates . . . will her humility hold her back? Just this once—Bernard tells her—do not be humble but daring! Give us your "yes"! This is the crucial moment when, from her lips, from her heart, the answer comes: "Let it be to me according to your word." It is the moment of free, humble yet magnanimous obedience in which the loftiest choice of human freedom is made.

Mary becomes a mother through her "yes." The Church Fathers sometimes expressed this by saying that Mary conceived through her ear—that is to say: through her hearing. Through her obedience, the Word entered into her and became fruitful in her. In this connection, the Fathers developed the idea of God's birth in us through faith and baptism, in which the *Lógos* comes to us ever anew, making us God's children. For example, we may recall the words of Saint Irenaeus: "How shall man pass into God, unless God has first passed into man? How was mankind to escape this birth into death, unless he were born again through faith, by that new birth from the Virgin, the sign of salvation that is God's wonderful and unmistakable gift?" (*Adv. Haer.* IV 33,4; cf. H. Rahner, *Our Lady and the Church*, p. 60).

I consider it important to focus also on the final sentence of Luke's annunciation narrative: "And the angel departed from her" (*Lk* 1:38). The great hour of Mary's encounter with God's messenger—in which her whole life is changed—comes to an end, and she remains there alone, with the task that truly surpasses all human capacity. There are no angels standing round her. She must continue along the path that leads through many dark moments—from Joseph's dismay at her pregnancy to the moment when Jesus is said to be out of his mind (cf. *Mk* 3:21; *Jn* 10:20), right up to the night of the Cross.

How often in these situations must Mary have returned inwardly to the hour when God's angel had spoken to her, pondering afresh the greeting: "Rejoice, full of grace!" and the consoling words: "Do not be afraid!" The angel departs; her mission remains, and with it matures her inner closeness to God, a closeness that in her heart she is able to see and touch.

THE CONCEPTION AND BIRTH OF JESUS ACCORDING TO MATTHEW

After considering Luke's annunciation narrative, we must now turn our attention to the tradition handed down in Matthew's Gospel regarding the same event. In contrast to Luke, Matthew relates it exclusively from the perspective of Saint Joseph, who as a descendant of David represents the link between the figure of Jesus and the Davidic promise.

Matthew begins by telling us that Mary was betrothed to Joseph. According to the prevailing Jewish law, betrothal already established a juridical bond between the two parties, so that Mary could be called Joseph's wife, even though he had not yet taken her into his home—the step which established the married state. While betrothed, "the woman still lived in her parents' home and remained under the *patria potestas*. After a year, her husband would take her into his home, thereby sealing the marriage" (Gnilka, *Das Matthäusevangelium,* p. 17). Now Joseph had to come to terms with the fact that Mary "was with child of the Holy Spirit" (*Mt* 1:18).

With regard to the child's origin, Matthew is anticipating something here that Joseph does not yet know. Joseph has to assume that Mary has broken their engagement, and according to the law he must dismiss her. He has a choice between a public juridical act and a private form. He can bring Mary before the court or he can issue her with a private writ of divorce. Joseph decides on the latter option, in order not "to put her to shame" (1:19). Matthew sees in this choice an indication that Joseph was "a just man."

The designation of Joseph as a just man (*zaddik*) extends far beyond the decision he takes at this moment: it gives an overall picture of Saint Joseph and at the same time it aligns him with the great figures of the Old Covenant—beginning with Abraham, the just. If we may say that the form of piety found in the New Testament can be summed up in the expression "a believer," then the Old Testament idea of a whole life lived according to sacred Scripture is summed up in the idea of "a just man."

Psalm 1 presents the classic image of the "just" man. We might well think of it as a portrait of the spiritual figure of Saint Joseph. A just man, it tells us, is one who maintains living contact with the word of God, who "delights in the law of the Lord" (v. 2). He is like a tree, planted beside the flowing waters, constantly bringing forth fruit. The flowing waters, from which he draws nourishment, naturally refer to the living word of God, into which he sinks the roots of his being. God's will is not a law imposed on him from without, it is "joy." For him the law is simply Gospel, good news, because he reads it with a personal, loving openness to God and in this way learns to understand and live it from deep within.

If Psalm 1 sees it as the mark of the just man, the "happy man," that he lives by the Torah, the word of God, the parallel passage in *Jer* 17:7 calls "blessed" the one "who puts his trust in the Lord, whose hope is the Lord." This text brings out more strongly than the psalm the personal character of righteousness—the trust in God that gives man hope. Although neither passage speaks explicitly of the "just" but rather of the "happy" or the "blessed," we may still regard them, with Hans-Joachim Kraus, as providing the authentic Old Testament image of the just man, and so we can learn from them what Matthew means when he describes Saint Joseph as "just."

This image of the man with roots in the living waters of God's word, whose life is spent in dialogue with God and who therefore brings forth constant fruit—this image becomes concrete in the event recounted here, as well as in everything we are subsequently told about Joseph of Nazareth. After the discovery that Joseph made, his task was to interpret and apply the law correctly. He does so with love: he does not want to give Mary up to public shame. He wishes her well, even in the hour of his great disappointment. He does not embody the form of externalized legalism that Jesus denounces in *Mt* 23 and that Paul opposes so strenuously. He lives the law as Gospel. He seeks the path that brings law and love into a unity. And so he is inwardly prepared for the new, unexpected and humanly speaking incredible news that comes to him from God.

Whereas the angel "came" to Mary (*Lk* 1:28), he merely appears to Joseph in a dream—admittedly a dream that is real and reveals what is real. Once again this shows us an essential quality of the figure of Saint Joseph: his capacity to perceive the divine and his ability to discern. Only a man who is inwardly watchful for the divine, only someone with a real sensitivity for God and his ways, can receive God's message in this way. And an ability to discern was necessary in order to know whether it was simply a dream or whether God's messenger had truly appeared to him and addressed him.

The message conveyed to Joseph is overwhelming, and it demands extraordinarily courageous faith. Can it be that God has really spoken, that what Joseph was told in the dream was the truth—a truth so far surpassing anything he could have foreseen? Can it be that God has acted in this way toward a human creature? Can it be that God has now launched a new history with men? Matthew has already said that Joseph "inwardly considered" (*enthymēthéntos*) the right way to respond to Mary's pregnancy. So we can well imagine his inner struggle now to make sense of this breathtaking dream-message: "Joseph, son of David, do not be afraid to take Mary your wife, for that which is conceived in her is of the Holy Spirit" (*Mt* 1:20).

Joseph is explicitly addressed as son of David, which also serves to indicate the task assigned to him in this event: as heir to the Davidic promise, he is to bear witness to God's faithfulness. "Do not be afraid" to take on this task, one that might well arouse fear. "Do not be afraid"—the very words that the angel of the annunciation had spoken to Mary. By means of this same exhortation from the angel, Joseph is now drawn into the mystery of God's incarnation.

After the message about the child's conception through the power of the Holy Spirit, Joseph is entrusted with a further task: "Mary will bear a son, and you shall call his name Jesus, for he will save his people from their sins" (*Mt* 1:21). Together with the instruction to take Mary as his wife, Joseph is asked to give a name to the child and thus legally to adopt it as his. It is the same name that the angel indicated to Mary as the name of the child: Jesus. The name Jesus (*Jeshua*) means "YHWH is salvation." The divine messenger who spoke to Joseph in the dream explains the nature of this salvation: "He will save his people from their sins."

On the one hand, then, a lofty theological task is assigned to the child, for only God can forgive sins. So this child is immediately associated with God, directly linked with

God's holy and saving power. On the other hand, though, this definition of the Messiah's mission could also appear disappointing. The prevailing expectations of salvation were primarily focused upon Israel's concrete sufferings— on the reestablishment of the Davidic kingdom, on Israel's freedom and independence, and naturally that included material prosperity for this largely impoverished people. The promise of forgiveness of sins seems both too little and too much: too much, because it trespasses upon God's exclusive sphere; too little, because there seems to be no thought of Israel's concrete suffering or its true need for salvation.

So this passage already anticipates the whole debate over Jesus' Messiahship: has he now redeemed Israel, or is everything still as it was before? Is the mission, as lived by Jesus, the answer to the promise, or is it not? Certainly it does not match the immediate expectations of Messianic salvation nurtured by men who felt oppressed not so much by their sins as by their sufferings, their lack of freedom, the wretched conditions of their existence.

Jesus himself poignantly raised the question as to where the priority lies in man's need for redemption on the occasion when the four men, who could not carry the paralytic through the door because of the crowd, let him down from the roof and laid him at Jesus' feet. The sick man's very existence was a plea, an urgent appeal for salvation, to which Jesus responded in a way that was quite contrary to the expectation of the bearers and of the sick man himself, saying: "My son, your sins are forgiven" (*Mk* 2:5). This was the last thing anyone was expecting. This was the last thing they were concerned about. The paralytic needed to be able to walk, not to be delivered from his sins. The scribes criticized the theological presumption of Jesus' words: the sick man and those around him were disappointed, because Jesus had apparently overlooked the man's real need.

I consider this whole scene to be of key significance for the question of Jesus' mission, in the terms with which it was first described in the angel's message to Joseph. In the passage concerned, both the criticism of the scribes and the silent expectation of the onlookers is acknowledged. Jesus then demonstrates his ability to forgive sins by ordering the sick man to take up his pallet and walk away healed. At the same time, the priority of forgiveness for sins as the foundation of all true healing is clearly maintained.

Man is a relational being. And if his first, fundamental relationship is disturbed—his relationship with God—then nothing else can be truly in order. This is where the priority lies in Jesus' message and ministry: before all else, he wants to point man toward the essence of his malady, and to show him—if you are not healed *there*, then however many good things you may find, you are not truly healed.

In this sense, the explanation of Jesus' name that was offered to Joseph in his dream already contains a fundamental clarification of how man's salvation has to be understood and hence what the Saviour's essential task must be.

After the angel's annunciation to Joseph of the virginal conception and birth of Jesus, Matthew adds two further statements that complete his narrative.

First he shows that these happenings had been foretold by the Scriptures. This is a characteristic feature of his Gospel: for all essential events, to adduce a "proof from Scripture"—to make it clear that the words of Scripture anticipate these events and inwardly prepare the way for them. Matthew demonstrates that the ancient words come true in the story of Jesus. But at the same time he shows that the story of Jesus is true: that is to say, it proceeds from the word of God, by which it is sustained and brought about.

After the Scriptural quotation, Matthew brings the story to a close. He recounts that Joseph awoke from sleep and did as the angel of the Lord had instructed him. He took Mary home as his wife, but did not "know" her until she had given birth to the Son. This underlines once more that the Son is begotten not from him but from the Holy Spirit. Finally the evangelist adds: "He called his name Jesus" (*Mt* 1:25).

Once again Joseph is presented to us, in quite practical terms, as a "just" man: his inner watchfulness for God, which enables him to receive and understand the message, leads quite spontaneously to obedience. Even if hitherto he had puzzled over his various options, now he knows what the right course of action is. Being a just man he follows God's commands, as Psalm 1 says.

At this point, we must examine the proof from Scripture that Matthew presents, which has become the object (how could it be otherwise?) of extensive exegetical debate. The verse is as follows: "All this took place to fulfill what the Lord had spoken by the prophet: 'Behold, a virgin shall conceive and bear a son, and his name shall be called Emmanuel,' which means, God with us" (*Mt* 1:22f.; cf. *Is* 7:14). This prophetic saying, which Matthew makes into one of the key Christological statements, we will first attempt to understand in its original historical context, and then we will try to see how the mystery of Jesus Christ is reflected in it.

Exceptionally, we are able to date this verse from Isaiah quite precisely. It comes from the year 733 B.C. The Assyrian King Tiglat-Pileser III had quashed the beginnings of an uprising by the Syro-Palestinian states by means of a surprise campaign. King Rezin of Damascus/Syria and King Pekah of Israel then formed a coalition against the great Assyrian power. Since they could not persuade King Ahaz of Judah to enter their alliance, they decided to take to the field against the Jerusalem king, in order to force his country into their coalition.

Understandably, Ahaz and his people were fearful in the face of the enemy alliance; the heart of the king and his people trembled "as the trees of the forest shake before the wind" (*Is* 7:2). Nevertheless Ahaz, who was evidently a clever and coldly calculating politician, maintained his previous line: he did not want to enter an anti-Assyrian alliance, which he evidently thought had no chance of success in view of the vast superiority of the superpower. Instead, he concluded a protection treaty with Assyria, which on the one hand guaranteed him security and saved his country from destruction, but on the other hand demanded, as a price, the worship of the protecting power's national gods.

After Ahaz had concluded the treaty with Assyria, despite Isaiah's warnings, an altar was indeed built on the Assyrian model in the Temple at Jerusalem (cf. 2 *Kings* 16:11ff.; cf. Kaiser, *Isaiah* 1–12, p. 149n.). At the time of the episode related in the Isaiah passage that Matthew quotes, this had yet to happen. But it was clear that if Ahaz was going to conclude this treaty with the great king of Assyria, it meant that as a politician he trusted more in the power of the king than in the power of God, which evidently did not strike him as sufficiently real. So what was at stake here was ultimately not a political problem, but a question of faith.

Isaiah tells the king that he need not fear the two "smoldering stumps of firebrands," Syria and Israel (Ephraim), and that there is therefore no reason for the protection treaty with Assyria: he should rely on faith, not on political calculations. Quite unconventionally, he invites Ahaz to request a sign from God, from the underworld or from the heights. The answer given by the king of Judah appears pious: he will not put God to the test and he will not ask for a sign (cf. *Is* 7:10–12). The prophet, speaking as God's mouthpiece, is not deterred. He knows that the king's refusal of the sign is not, as it appears, an expression of faith, but on the contrary an indication that he does not want to be disturbed in his *Realpolitik*.

So now the prophet declares that the Lord himself will give a sign: "Behold, a virgin shall conceive and bear a son, and shall call his name Emmanuel" (God with us—*Is* 7:14).

What is the sign promised to Ahaz in this passage? Matthew, and with him the entire Christian tradition, sees in it a prophecy of the birth of Jesus from the Virgin Mary: even though Jesus is not actually named Emmanuel, nevertheless he *is* Emmanuel, as the entire history of the Gospels seeks to demonstrate. This man—they tell us—in his very person is God's being-with-men. He is true man and at the same time God, God's true Son.

But is that how Isaiah understood the prophetic sign? Against this it is rightly objected, in the first place, that the sign announced to Ahaz was intended for him *there and then*, and was meant to stir him to faith in the God of Israel as the true ruler of the world. So the sign would need to be sought and identified within the historical context in which it was announced by the prophet. Exegesis has therefore searched meticulously, using all the resources of historical scholarship, for a contemporary interpretation—and it has failed.

Rudolf Kilian, in his commentary on Isaiah, briefly describes the essential attempts that have been made. He speaks of four principal types of interpretation. The first is this: "Emmanuel" refers to the Messiah. Yet the idea of the Messiah only reached its fully developed form at the time of the Exile and thereafter. Here at most we could be dealing with an anticipation of this figure: there is nothing contemporary with Isaiah that might correspond to it. The second hypothesis assumes that the "God with us" is a son of King Ahaz, perhaps Hezekiah—a thesis that simply does not add up. The third theory suggests that it refers to one of the sons of the prophet Isaiah, both of whom have prophetic names (*Shear-jashub*: "a remnant shall return" and *Maher-Shalal-Hash-Baz*: "the spoil speeds, the prey hastens"; cf. *Is* 7:3; 8:3), but this attempt does not add up either. A fourth thesis argues for a collective interpretation: Emmanuel as the new Israel, and the *'almāh* ("virgin") as "none other than the symbolic figure of Zion." But the context of the prophet in no way points toward a notion of this kind, and in any event, such a sign could not be historically contemporary. Kilian concludes his analysis of the various exegetical approaches as follows: "As a result of this overview it turns out that no single attempt at interpretation is entirely convincing. The mother and child remain a mystery, at least to the modern reader, but probably also to the contemporary audience, perhaps even to the prophet himself" (*Jesaja 1–12*, p. 62).

So what are we to say? The passage about the virgin who gives birth to Emmanuel, like the great Suffering Servant song in *Is* 53, is a word in waiting. There is nothing in its own historical context to correspond to it. So it remains an open question: it is addressed not merely to Ahaz. Nor is it addressed merely to Israel. It is addressed to humanity. The sign that God himself announces is given not for a specific political situation, but it concerns the whole history of humanity.

Should Christians not hear this word as their own? On listening to this verse, should they not come to the conviction that the message which always seemed so strange, waiting to be deciphered, has now come true? Should they not be convinced that God has now given us this sign in the birth of Jesus from the Virgin Mary? Emmanuel has come. Marius Reiser has summed up the way Christian readers have experienced this passage as follows: "The prophet's prediction is like a miraculously formed keyhole, into which the key of Christ fits perfectly" (*Bibelkritik*, p. 328).

Indeed, I believe that in our own day, after all the efforts of critical exegesis, we can share anew this sense of astonishment at the fact that a saying from the year 733 B.C., incomprehensible for so long, came true at the moment of the conception of Jesus Christ—that God did indeed give us a great sign intended for the whole world.

VIRGIN BIRTH——MYTH OR HISTORICAL TRUTH?

Finally we must ask in all seriousness: when the evangelists Matthew and Luke tell us, in their different ways and following different traditions, about Jesus' conception from the Virgin Mary by the power of the Holy Spirit, is this a historical reality, a real historical event, or is it a pious legend, which seeks to express and interpret the mystery of Jesus in its own way?

Especially since Eduard Norden († 1941) and Martin Dibelius († 1947), attempts have been made to explain the account of Jesus' virgin birth in terms of the history of religions, and the stories of the conception and birth of the Egyptian Pharaohs seem to have been hailed as a particularly important discovery in this regard. A second set of related ideas has been identified in early Judaism, again in Egypt, in the writings of Philo of Alexandria († after 40 A.D.). The two sets of ideas are nevertheless very different from one another. The narrative of the divine generation of the Pharaohs, which involves the deity physically approaching the mother, is ultimately about giving theological legitimacy to the cult of the ruler, it is a political theology that seeks to raise the king into the realm of the divine and thus to legitimize his divine claims. Philo's account of the generation of the sons of the patriarchs from divine seed, on the other hand, is allegorical in character. "The wives of the patriarchs . . . become allegories for the virtues. As such they become pregnant from God, and they give birth for their husbands to the virtues that they themselves embody" (Gnilka, *Das Matthäusevangelium*, p. 25). It is hard to know to what extent, over and above allegory, any concrete interpretation is intended.

On careful reading, it is clear that neither case offers a real parallel to the account of Jesus' virgin birth. The same applies to texts from the Graeco-Roman world, which some have wanted to cite as pagan models for the story of Jesus' conception through the Holy Spirit: the liaison between Zeus and Alcmene that led to the birth of Heracles, or that between Zeus and Danaë, from which Perseus was born, and so on.

The difference between the concepts involved is so profound that one really cannot speak of true parallels. In the Gospel accounts, the oneness of the one God and the infinite distance between God and creature is fully preserved. There is no mixture, no demi-god. It is God's creative word alone that brings about something new. Jesus, born of Mary, is fully man and fully God, without confusion and without separation, as the creed of Chalcedon in the year 451 was to clarify.

The accounts of Matthew and Luke are not myths taken a stage further. They are firmly rooted, in terms of their basic conception, in the biblical tradition of God the Creator and Redeemer. As far as their specific content is concerned, though, they are derived from the family tradition, they are a tradition handed down, recording the events that took place.

I tend to regard as the one true explanation of these stories something that Joachim Gnilka, following Gerhard Delling, expressed as a question: "Might the mystery surrounding the birth of Jesus . . . be a later addition prefixed to the Gospel, or does it not rather serve to indicate that the mystery was already known? It is just that there was a desire not to say too much about it, or to reduce it to an event like any other" (*Das Matthäusevangelium*, p. 30).

It seems natural to me that only after Mary's death could the mystery be made public and pass into the shared patrimony of early Christianity. At that point it could find its way into the evolving complex of Christological doctrine and be linked to the confession of Jesus as the Christ, the Son of God—yet not in the manner of a story crafted from an idea, an idea reformulated as a fact, but vice versa: the event itself, a fact that was now in the public domain, became the object of reflection—understanding was sought. The overall picture of Jesus Christ shed light upon the event, and conversely, through that event, the divine logic was more deeply grasped. The mystery of his origin illuminated what came later, and conversely the developed form of Christological faith helped to make sense of that origin. Thus did Christology develop.

Perhaps it is appropriate at this point to mention a text which from earliest times has fascinated Western Christianity as a possible intuition of the mystery of the virgin birth. I am thinking of Virgil's Fourth Eclogue from his poetic cycle *Bucolics* (Pastoral Poems), written about forty years before the birth of Jesus. In among these playful verses on rural life, suddenly a very different tone is sounded: the birth of a new great world order from that which is "undefiled" (*ab integro*) is proclaimed. "*Iam redit et virgo*—now the virgin returns." A new generation descends from heaven on high. A boy is born, with whom the "iron" brood ends.

What is being promised here? Who is the virgin? Who is the boy that is spoken of? Here too, as in the case of *Is* 7:14, scholars have tried to make historical identifications, which have likewise run into difficulties. So what is being said? The overall conceptual framework comes from the worldview of antiquity: in the background is the doctrine of the cycles of the aeons and the force of destiny. But these ancient concepts take on a fresh contemporary aspect with the expectation that the time has now come for a great new aeon to begin. What had hitherto been only a remote prediction suddenly moves into the present. In the age of Augustus, after the great upheavals of war and civil strife, a wave of hope surges through the land: now at last a great period of peace, a new world order, seems about to dawn.

Linked to this sense of change in the air is the figure of the virgin, the image of the pure, undefiled one, the fresh start *ab integro*. So too is the expectation of the boy, the "offspring of the gods" (*deum suboles*). Hence, one could say that the figures of the virgin and the divine child belong in some sense to the archetypal images of human hope, which emerge at times of crisis and expectation, even without there being any concrete figures in view.

Let us return to the biblical accounts of the birth of Jesus from the Virgin Mary, who had conceived the child by the Holy Spirit. Is it true? Or is it possible that archetypal concepts have been transferred onto the figures of Jesus and his mother?

Anyone who reads the biblical accounts and compares them to the related traditions mentioned above will immediately notice the profound difference. Not only the comparison with Egyptian models, of which we have spoken, but also the dream of hope that we encountered in Virgil point toward very different worlds.

In Matthew and Luke there is no trace of a cosmic revolution, nor is there any physical encounter between God and human beings: what we read there is an utterly humble story, yet one whose very humility gives it a disturbing grandeur. It is Mary's obedience that opens the door to God. God's word, his Spirit, creates the child in her. He does so through the door of her obedience. In this way, Jesus is the new Adam, the new beginning *ab integro*—from the Virgin, who places herself entirely at the disposal of God's will. So a new creation comes about, which is nevertheless tied to the free "yes" of the human creature, Mary.

Perhaps one could say that humanity's silent and confused dreams of a new beginning came true in this event—in a reality such that only God could create.

Is what we profess in the Creed true, then?—"I believe in one Lord Jesus Christ, the Only Begotten Son of God . . . [who] by the Holy Spirit was incarnate of the Virgin Mary"?

The answer is an unequivocal yes. Karl Barth pointed out that there are two moments in the story of Jesus when God intervenes directly in the material world: the virgin birth and the resurrection from the tomb, in which Jesus did not remain, nor see corruption. These two moments are a scandal to the modern spirit. God is "allowed" to act in ideas and thoughts, in the spiritual domain—but not in the material. That is shocking. He does not belong there. But that is precisely the point: God is God and he does not operate merely on the level of ideas. In that sense, what is at stake in both of these moments is God's very godhead. The question that they raise is: does matter also belong to him?

Naturally we may not ascribe to God anything nonsensical or irrational, or anything that contradicts his creation. But here we are not dealing with the irrational or contradictory, but precisely with the positive—with God's creative power, embracing the whole of being. In that sense these two moments—the virgin birth and the real resurrection from the tomb—are the cornerstones of faith. If God does not also have power over matter, then he simply is not God. But he does have this power, and through the conception and resurrection of Jesus Christ he has ushered in a new creation. So as the Creator he is also our Redeemer. Hence the conception and birth of Jesus from the Virgin Mary is a fundamental element of our faith and a radiant sign of hope.

CHAPTER III

The Birth of Jesus in Bethlehem

THE HISTORICAL AND THEOLOGICAL FRAMEWORK OF THE NATIVITY STORY IN LUKE'S GOSPEL

"In those days a decree went out from Caesar Augustus that all the world should be enrolled" (*Lk* 2:1). With these words, Luke introduces his account of the birth of Jesus and explains how it came to take place in Bethlehem. A population census, for purposes of determining and collecting taxes, was what prompted Joseph to set off from Nazareth for Bethlehem, together with Mary, his betrothed, who was expecting a child. The birth of Jesus in the city of David is placed within the overarching framework of world history, even though Caesar was quite unaware of the difficult journey that these ordinary people were making on his account. And so it is that the child Jesus is born, seemingly by chance, in the place of the promise.

The context in world history is important for Luke. For

the first time, "all the world," the *ecumēnē* in its entirety, is to be enrolled. For the first time there is a government and an empire that spans the globe. For the first time, there is a great expanse of peace in which everyone's property can be registered and placed at the service of the wider community. Only now, when there is a commonality of law and property on a large scale, and when a universal language has made it possible for a cultural community to trade in ideas and goods, only now can a message of universal salvation, a universal Saviour, enter the world: it is indeed the "fullness of time."

Yet the link between Jesus and Augustus goes deeper. Augustus did not want merely to be a ruler like any other, such as had existed before him and would come after him. The inscription at Priene, from the year 9 B.C., helps us to understand how he wanted to be seen and understood. There it is said that the day of the Emperor's birth "gave the whole world a new aspect. It would have fallen into ruin had not a widespread well-being shone forth through him, the one now born . . . Providence, which has ordered all things, filled this man with virtue that he might benefit mankind, sending him as a Saviour (*sōtēr*) both for us and our descendants . . . The birthday of the god was the beginning of the good tidings that he brought for the world. From his birth, a new reckoning of time must begin" (cf. Stöger, *Lukasevangelium*, p. 74).

From a text like this it is clear that Augustus was regarded not just as a politician, but as a theological figure—which shows that our distinction between politics and religion, between politics and theology, simply did not exist in the ancient world. In the year 27 B.C., three years after his assumption of office, the Roman Senate had already awarded him the title *Augustus* (in Greek: *sebastós*)—meaning "one worthy of adoration." In the inscription at Priene, he is called Saviour, Redeemer (*sōtēr*). This title, which literature ascribed to Zeus, but also to Epicurus and Asclepius, is reserved in the Greek translation of the Old Testament to God alone. For Augustus too, there was a divine ring to it: the Emperor ushered in a changed world, a new era.

In Virgil's Fourth Eclogue, we have already encountered the hope of a new world, the expectation of a return to Paradise. While in Virgil, as we have seen, there is a broader background to this, nevertheless the outlook on life typical of the Augustan era leaves its mark: "Now all must change . . ."

There are two aspects of the self-understanding of Augustus and his contemporaries that I would like to single out. Peace, above all, was what the "Saviour" brought to the world. Augustus himself left a lasting monument to his peace-bringing mission in the *Ara Pacis Augusti*, the remains of which, even today, manifest most impressively how the universal peace that he established for a certain period made it possible to breathe freely and to hope. Marius Reiser, citing Antonie Wlosok, writes as follows: On 23 September (the Emperor's birthday), "between morning and evening, the shadow of this sun clock moved about 150m straight along the equinox, to the very centre of the *Ara Pacis*; there is thus a direct line from the birth of this man to *Pax*, and in this way it is clearly demonstrated that he is *natus ad pacem* (born for peace). The shadow comes from a ball, and the ball . . . is both the heavenly sphere and the earthly globe, a symbol of dominion over the world which is now at peace" (*Wie wahr*, p. 459).

Here we see the second aspect of Augustus' self-image: the universality that, once again, he himself put on display in a very public record of his life and work, listing specific facts—the so-called *Monumentum Ancyranum*.

This brings us back to the registration of all the inhabitants of the empire, by which the birth of Jesus of Nazareth is linked to Caesar Augustus. There is a long-running dispute among experts regarding this tax collection (population census), but there is no need for us to enter into all the details here.

One initial problem can be solved quite easily: the census took place at the time of King Herod the Great, who actually died in the year 4 B.C. The starting-point for our reckoning of time—the calculation of Jesus' date of birth—

goes back to the monk Dionysius Exiguus († c. 550), who evidently miscalculated by a few years. The historical date of the birth of Jesus is therefore to be placed a few years earlier.

There is much debate regarding the date of the census. According to Flavius Josephus, to whom we owe most of our knowledge of Jewish history around the time of Jesus, it took place in the year 6 A.D. under the governor Quirinius, and as it was ultimately a question of money, it led to the uprising of Judas the Galilean (cf. *Acts* 5:37). According to Josephus it was only then, and not before, that Quirinius was active in the region of Syria and Judea. Yet these claims in their turn are uncertain. At any rate, there are indications that Quirinius was already in the Emperor's service in Syria around 9 B.C. So it is most illuminating when such scholars as Alois Stöger suggest that the "population census" was a slow process in the conditions of the time, dragging on over several years. Moreover, it was implemented in two stages: firstly, registration of all land and property ownership, and then—in the second phase—determination of the payments that were due. The first stage would have taken place at the time of Jesus' birth; the second, much more injurious for the people, was what provoked the uprising (cf. Stöger, *Lukasevangelium*, pp. 372f.).

Some have raised the further objection that there was no need, in a census of this kind, for each person to travel to his hometown (cf. *Lk* 2:3). But we also know from various sources that those affected had to present themselves where they owned property. Accordingly, we may assume that Joseph, of the house of David, had property in Bethlehem, so that he had to go there for tax registration.

Regarding the details, the discussion could continue indefinitely. It is difficult to gain an insight into the daily life of a society so complex and so distant from our own as that of the Roman Empire. Yet the essential content of Luke's narrative remains historically credible all the same: Luke set out, as he says in the prologue to his Gospel, "to write an orderly account" (1:3). This he evidently did, making use of the means at his disposal. In any case, he was situated much closer to the sources and events than we could ever claim to be, despite all our historical scholarship.

Let us return to the wider context of the moment in history when Jesus' birth took place. By referring to the Emperor Augustus and to "the whole *ecumēnē*," Luke was intentionally creating both a historical and a theological framework for the events he was about to recount.

Jesus was born at a time that can be precisely determined. Later, at the start of Jesus' public ministry, Luke once again offers a meticulously detailed chronology of that particular moment in history: the fifteenth year of the reign of the Emperor Tiberius. He adds the names of the Roman governor that year, the tetrarchs of Galilee, of Ituraea and Trachonitis and of Abilene, as well as the high-priests (cf. *Lk* 3:1f.).

It was not with the timelessness of myth that Jesus came to be born among us. He belongs to a time that can be precisely dated and a geographical area that is precisely defined: here the universal and the concrete converge. It was in him that the *Lógos*, the creative logic behind all things, entered the world. The eternal *Lógos* became man: the context of place and time is part of this. Faith attaches itself to this concrete reality, even if the resurrection then bursts open the categories of time and space, as the risen Lord, going before the disciples into Galilee (cf. *Mt* 28:7), opens up a pathway into the vast expanse of humanity (cf. *Mt* 28:16ff.).

There is a further important element. Augustus' instruction regarding the registration, for tax purposes, of all the citizens of the *ecumēnē* leads Joseph, together with Mary, his betrothed, to Bethlehem, the city of David, and thus it helps to bring to fulfillment the promise of the prophet Micah that the shepherd of Israel would be born in that city (cf. 5:1–3). The Emperor unwittingly contributes to the realization of the prophecy: the history of the Roman Empire is interwoven with the history of the salvation that God established with Israel. The history of God's election, hitherto confined to Israel, enters the wider world, it enters world history. God, who is the God of Israel and of all peoples, shows himself to be the true guiding force behind all history.

Significant exponents of modern exegesis take the view that when Matthew and Luke say Jesus was born in Bethlehem, they are making a theological statement, not a historical one. In actual fact, these exegetes claim, Jesus was born in Nazareth. By placing the birth of Jesus in Bethlehem, the evangelists are thought to have refashioned history theologically, in accordance with the promises, so as to make it possible to designate Jesus, on the basis of his birthplace, as the long-awaited shepherd of Israel (cf. *Mic* 5:1–3; *Mt* 2:6).

I do not see how a basis for this theory can be gleaned from the actual sources. As far as the birth of Jesus is concerned, the only sources we have are the infancy narratives of Matthew and Luke. The two evidently belong to quite distinct narrative traditions. They are marked by different theological visions, just as their historical details are in some respects different.

Matthew apparently did not know that Joseph and Mary were both originally from Nazareth. Hence, on returning from Egypt, Joseph initially wants to go to Bethlehem, and it is only the news that a son of Herod is reigning in Judea that causes him to travel to Galilee instead. For Luke, on the other hand, it is clear from the outset that the holy family returned to Nazareth after the events surrounding the birth. The two different strands of tradition agree on the fact that Bethlehem was Jesus' birthplace. If we abide by the sources, it is clear that Jesus was born in Bethlehem and grew up in Nazareth.

THE BIRTH OF JESUS

"And while they were there [in Bethlehem], the time came for her to be delivered. And she gave birth to her first-born son and wrapped him in swaddling cloths, and laid him in a manger, because there was no room for them in the inn" (*Lk* 2:6f.).

Let us begin our exegesis with the concluding words of this passage: there was no room for them in the inn. Prayerful reflection over these words has highlighted an inner parallel between this saying and the profoundly moving verse from Saint John's Prologue: "He came to his own home, and his own people received him not" (1:11). For the Saviour of the world, for him in whom all things were created (cf. *Col* 1:16), there was no room. "Foxes have holes, and birds of the air have nests; but the Son of man has nowhere to lay his head" (*Mt* 8:20). He who was crucified outside the city (cf. *Heb* 13:12) also came into the world outside the city.

This should cause us to reflect—it points toward the reversal of values found in the figure of Jesus Christ and his message. From the moment of his birth, he belongs outside the realm of what is important and powerful in worldly terms. Yet it is this unimportant and powerless child that proves to be the truly powerful one, the one on whom ultimately everything depends. So one aspect of becoming a Christian is having to leave behind what everyone else thinks and wants, the prevailing standards, in order to enter the light of the truth of our being, and aided by that light to find the right path.

Mary laid her newborn child in a manger (cf. *Lk* 2:7). From this detail it has been correctly deduced that Jesus was born in a stable, in an inhospitable—one might even say unworthy—space, which nevertheless provided the necessary privacy for the sacred event. In the area around Bethlehem, rocky caves had been used as stables since ancient times (cf. Stuhlmacher, *Die Geburt des Immanuel*, p. 51).

As early as Justin Martyr († 165) and Origen († c. 254), we find the tradition that Jesus was born in a cave, which Christians in Palestine could point to. The fact that after the expulsion of the Jews from the Holy Land in the second century, Rome turned the cave into a shrine of Tammuz-Adonis, thereby evidently intending to suppress the Christian memorial cult, confirms the age of this shrine and also shows how important it was thought to be by the Romans. Local traditions are frequently a more reliable source than written records. So a considerable measure of credibility may be assigned to the tradition that Bethlehem was Jesus' birthplace, a tradition to which the Church of the Nativity also bears witness.

Mary wrapped the child in swaddling cloths. Without yielding to sentimentality, we may imagine with what great love Mary approached her hour and prepared for the birth of her child. Iconographic tradition has theologically interpreted the manger and the swaddling cloths in terms of the theology of the Fathers. The child stiffly wrapped in bandages is seen as prefiguring the hour of his death: from the outset, he is the sacrificial victim, as we shall see more closely when we examine the reference to the first-born. The manger, then, was seen as a kind of altar.

Augustine drew out the meaning of the manger using an idea that at first seems almost shocking, but on closer examination contains a profound truth. The manger is the place where animals find their food. But now, lying in the manger, is he who called himself the true bread come down from heaven, the true nourishment that we need in order to be fully ourselves. This is the food that gives us true life, eternal life. Thus the manger becomes a reference to the table of God, to which we are invited so as to receive the bread of God. From the poverty of Jesus' birth emerges the miracle in which man's redemption is mysteriously accomplished.

The manger, as we have seen, indicates animals, who come to it for their food. In the Gospel there is no reference to animals at this point. But prayerful reflection, reading Old and New Testaments in the light of one another, filled this lacuna at a very early stage by pointing to *Is* 1:3: "The ox knows its owner, and the ass its master's crib; but Israel does not know, my people does not understand."

Peter Stuhlmacher points out that the Greek version of *Hab* 3:2 may well have contributed here: "In the midst of two living creatures you will be recognized . . . when the time has come, you will appear" (cf. *Die Geburt des Immanuel*, p. 52). The two living creatures would appear to refer to the two cherubs on the mercy-seat of the Ark of the Covenant (cf. *Ex* 25:18–20), who both reveal and conceal the mysterious presence of God. So the manger has in some sense become the Ark of the Covenant, in which God is mysteriously hidden among men, and before which the time has come for "ox and ass"—humanity made up of Jews and Gentiles—to acknowledge God.

Through this remarkable combination of *Is* 1:3, *Hab* 3:2, *Ex* 25:18–20 and the manger, the two animals now appear as an image of a hitherto blind humanity which now, before the child, before God's humble self-manifestation in the stable, has learned to recognize him, and in the lowliness of his birth receives the revelation that now teaches all people to see. Christian iconography adopted this motif at an early stage. No representation of the crib is complete without the ox and the ass.

After this brief digression, let us return to the text of the Gospel. "Mary gave birth to her first-born son," we read in *Lk* 2:7. What does this mean?

The first-born is not necessarily the first in a series. The word "first-born" points not to a continuing number, but rather indicates a theological quality which finds expression in the oldest of Israel's collections of laws. The instructions for the Passover contain the following passages: "The Lord said to Moses: 'Consecrate to me all the first-born; whatever is the first to open the womb among the people of Israel, both of man and of beast, is mine'" (*Ex* 13:1f.). "Every first-born of man among your sons you shall redeem" (*Ex* 13:13). So the reference to the first-born is also an anticipation of the account, soon to follow, of Jesus' presentation in the Temple. Clearly, this word highlights the particular way in which Jesus belongs to God.

Pauline theology took the idea of Jesus as first-born two steps further. In the Letter to the Romans, Paul calls Jesus the "first-born among many brethren" (8:29). Having risen, he is now "first-born" in a new way, and at the same time he is the beginning of a host of brethren. In the new birth of the resurrection, Jesus is no longer merely the first in dignity, he now ushers in a new humanity. Once he has broken through the iron door of death, there are many more who can pass through with him—many who in baptism have died with him and risen with him.

In the Letter to the Colossians, the idea is developed further: Christ is called "first-born of all creation" (1:15) and "first-born from the dead" (1:18). "In him all things were created" (1:16), "that in everything he might be pre-eminent" (1:18). The concept of first-born takes on a cosmic dimension. Christ, the incarnate Son, is—so to speak—God's first thought, preceding all creation, which is ordered toward him and proceeds from him. He is both the beginning and the goal of the new creation that was initiated with the resurrection.

Luke does not speak in these terms, yet for us, reading his Gospel with the benefit of hindsight, this cosmic glory is already present in the lowly manger in the cave at Bethlehem: here, he who is truly the first-born of all that is, came to dwell in our midst.

"And in that region there were shepherds out in the field, keeping watch over their flocks by night. And an angel of the Lord appeared to them, and the glory of the Lord shone around them" (Lk 2:8f.). The first witnesses of the great event are watchful shepherds. There has been much reflection on the significance of the fact that shepherds were the first to receive the message. It seems to me that we should not read too much into this. Jesus was born outside the city in an area surrounded by grazing grounds where shepherds would pasture their flocks. So it was natural that, as the people physically closest to the event, they would be the first to be summoned to the manger.

Of course one could immediately develop this idea further: perhaps they were living not only outwardly but also inwardly closer to the event than the peacefully sleeping townsfolk. Inwardly too, they were not far from the God who had become a child. What is more, they were among the poor, the simple souls whom Jesus would bless, because to them above all is granted access to the mystery of God (cf. *Lk* 10:21f.). They represent the *poor of Israel*, the poor in general: God's first love.

Another element has been particularly emphasized by the monastic tradition: the shepherds' watchfulness. Monks set out to be watchful in this world—in the first place through their nocturnal prayer, but above all inwardly, open to receiving God's call through the signs of his presence.

Finally we may allude to the story of how David was chosen to be king. King Saul is rejected by God, and Samuel is sent to Bethlehem, to Jesse, to anoint as king one of his sons, whom the Lord will point out. None of the sons who appear before Samuel is the one. The youngest is still absent, but he is looking after the sheep, as Jesse explains to the prophet. Samuel has him fetched from the fields, and at God's indication, he anoints the young David "in the midst of his brothers" (cf. 1 *Sam* 16:1–13). David comes from looking after the sheep, and he is made the shepherd of Israel (cf. 2 *Sam* 5:2). The prophet Micah, gazing far into the future, announces that from Bethlehem will come the one who is to pasture the people of Israel (cf. 5:1–3; *Mt* 2:6). Jesus is born among shepherds. He is the great Shepherd of mankind (cf. 1 *Pet* 2:25; *Heb* 13:20).

Let us return to the text of the Christmas story. The angel of the Lord appears to the shepherds and the glory of the Lord shines around them. "They were filled with fear" (*Lk* 2:9). But the angel takes away their fear and announces to them "a great joy, which will come to all the people; for to you is born this day in the city of David a Saviour, who is Christ the Lord" (*Lk* 2:10f.). They are told that, as a sign, they will find a child wrapped in swaddling cloths and lying in a manger.

"And suddenly there was with the angel a multitude of the heavenly host praising God and saying, 'Glory to God in the highest, and on earth peace among men with whom he is pleased'" (*Lk* 2:12–14). According to the evangelist, the angels "said" this. But Christianity has always understood that the speech of angels is actually song, in which all the glory of the great joy that they proclaim becomes tangibly present. And so, from that moment, the angels' song of praise has never gone silent. It continues down the centuries in constantly new forms and it resounds ever anew at the celebration of Jesus' birth. It is only natural that simple believers would then hear the shepherds singing too, and to this day they join in their caroling on the Holy Night, proclaiming in song the great joy that, from then until the end of time, is bestowed on all people.

What was it, though, according to Saint Luke's account, that the angels sang? They link God's glory "in the highest" with peace among men "on earth." The Church has taken up these words and crafted an entire hymn from them. In matters of detail, one has to admit, there is disagreement over how best to translate the angels' words.[1]

The familiar Latin text was until recently rendered thus: "Glory be to God on high and on earth peace to men of good will." This translation has been rejected by modern exegetes—not without reason—as one-sided and moralizing. "God's glory" is not something to be brought about by men ("Glory *be* to God"). The "glory" of God is real, God *is* glorious, and this is truly a reason for joy: there *is* truth, there *is* goodness, there *is* beauty. It is there—in God— indestructibly.

Of greater significance are the differences in translation of the second half of the angels' song. What was previously translated as "men of good will" is now rendered in the translation of the German Bishops' Conference "*Menschen seiner Gnade* [men of his grace]." In the translation of the

---

[1] Translator's Note: It should be noted that in what follows, the author is chiefly concerned with the translation into German of the Greek text of *Lk* 2:14.

Italian Bishops' Conference, the text reads *"uomini che egli ama* [men that he loves]." Here the question naturally arises: which men does God love? Are there any that he does not love? Does he not love them all as his creatures? What is added by the words "that God loves"? A similar question could be asked regarding the German translation. Who are the "men of his grace"? Are there any who are not in his grace? And if not, why not? The literal translation of the original Greek reads: peace "to men of good pleasure [= to men with whom he is pleased]." Here too the question obviously arises: which men enjoy God's "good pleasure"? And why?

Now, with regard to this question, the New Testament itself provides an aid to understanding. In the account of Jesus' baptism, Luke tells us that as Jesus was praying, the heavens opened and a voice came from heaven, saying: "You are my beloved Son; with you I am well pleased [= *I have good pleasure*]" (3:22). The man "with whom he is pleased" is Jesus. And the reason for this is that Jesus lives completely oriented toward the Father, focused upon him and in communion of will with him. So men "with whom he is pleased" are those who share the attitude of the Son—those who are conformed to Christ.

Behind the differences in translation, what is ultimately at stake here is the relationship between God's grace and human freedom. Two extreme positions are possible: firstly, the idea of the absolutely exclusive action of God, in which everything depends on his predestination. At the other extreme, there is a moralizing position, according to which everything is ultimately decided through the good will of the human person. The older translation—men "of good will"—could be misconstrued in this direction. The new translation can be misinterpreted in the opposite direction, as if everything depended uniquely on God's predestination.

The overall testimony of sacred Scripture demonstrates beyond doubt that neither of the two extreme positions is correct. Grace and freedom are thoroughly interwoven, and we cannot unravel their interrelatedness into clear formulae. It remains true that we could not love if we were not first loved by God. God's grace always precedes us, embraces us and carries us. But it also remains true that man is called to love in return, he does not remain an unwilling tool of God's omnipotence: he can love in return or he can refuse God's love. It seems to me that the literal translation—"of good pleasure" (or "of his good pleasure")—captures this mystery most fully, without resolving it one-sidedly.

As far as "glory in the highest" is concerned, the key word is the indicative "is."[2] God *is* glorious, he *is* indestructible truth, eternal beauty. That is the fundamental, comforting security of our faith. Yet this also contains an implicit

---

[2] Translator's Note: The German text to which the author refers, literally translated into English, would read: "God is glorified in the highest, and there is peace on earth . . ."

imperative to us, corresponding to the first three commandments of the Decalogue: to ensure that God's great glory is not sullied or distorted in the world, that his greatness and his holy will are held in honor.

At this point, we must consider a further aspect of the angels' message. It brings us back to the fundamental categories of Caesar Augustus' self-understanding and worldview: *sōtēr* (Saviour), peace, *ecumēnē*—this time, though, reaching beyond the Mediterranean region to encompass heaven and earth—and finally, the word applied to the good news itself *(euangélion)*. These parallels are by no means coincidental. Luke intends to say that what Caesar Augustus claimed for himself is realized in a loftier way in the defenseless and powerless child born in a Bethlehem cave and visited by poor shepherds.

Reiser rightly emphasizes that at the heart of both messages is peace, and that the *Pax Christi* is not necessarily opposed to the *Pax Augusti*. Yet the peace of Christ surpasses the peace of Augustus as heaven surpasses earth (cf. *Wie wahr*, p. 460). Hence the juxtaposition of these two forms of peace need not be seen in a one-sidedly polemical way. Augustus truly brought "peace, security of law and prosperity for 250 years, which many countries of the former Roman Empire can only dream of today" *(ibid., p. 458).* Politics retains its own sphere of competence and responsibility. And yet when

Caesar claims divine status and divine attributes, politics oversteps its boundaries and makes promises that it cannot deliver. And it must be acknowledged that, even at the height of the Roman Empire, security of law, peace and prosperity were never entirely unthreatened and never completely realized. One need only look to the Holy Land to see the limits of the *Pax Romana*.

The kingdom that Jesus proclaimed, the kingdom of God, is of another kind. It applies not just to the Mediterranean region and not just to a particular era. It applies to man in the depths of his being, and it opens him toward the true God. The peace of Jesus is a peace that the world cannot give (cf. *Jn* 14:27). Ultimately, the question here is what redemption, liberation and salvation actually mean. One thing is clear, though: Augustus belongs to the past, Jesus Christ on the other hand is the present and the future—he is "the same yesterday and today and for ever" (*Heb* 13:8).

"When the angels went away from them . . . the shepherds said to one another, 'Let us go over to Bethlehem and see this thing that has happened, which the Lord has made known to us.' And they went with haste, and found Mary and Joseph, and the babe lying in a manger" (*Lk* 2:15f.). The shepherds made haste. In a similar way, the evangelist had said that Mary, on receiving the angel's message about her cousin

Elizabeth's pregnancy, went "with haste" to the town in Judea where Zechariah and Elizabeth lived (cf. *Lk* 1:39). The shepherds made haste, partly no doubt from human curiosity, in order to see this great thing that had been announced to them. But surely, too, they were driven by their joy on hearing that now, truly, the Saviour, the Messiah, the Lord had been born, the one so long awaited—and they would be the first to see him.

How many Christians make haste today, where the things of God are concerned? Surely if anything merits haste—so the evangelist is discreetly telling us—then it is the things of God.

As a sign, the angel had told the shepherds that they would find a child wrapped in swaddling cloths and lying in a manger. This is an identifying sign—a description of what they would see. It is not a "sign" in the sense that God's glory would be rendered visible, so that one might say unequivocally: this is the true Lord of the world. Far from it. In this sense, the sign is also a non-sign. God's poverty is his real sign. But for the shepherds, who had seen God's glory shining in their fields, this is sign enough. They see inwardly. They see that the angel's words are true. So the shepherds return home with joy. They glorify God and praise him for what they have heard and seen (cf. *Lk* 2:20).

The presentation of Jesus in the Temple

Luke concludes the narrative of Jesus' birth with an account of what happened to him, in accordance with Israel's law, on the eighth day and on the fortieth day.

The eighth day is the day of circumcision, when Jesus is formally taken up into the community of the promises extending back to Abraham: now he is legally a member of the people of Israel. Paul speaks of this event when he writes to the Galatians: "But when the time had fully come, God sent forth his Son, born of woman, born under the law, to redeem those who were under the law, so that we might receive adoption as sons" (4:4f.). In addition to the circumcision, Luke expressly mentions the naming of the child (2:21) with the name that had been foretold—Jesus ("God saves")—so that from the circumcision, the reader's gaze is opened up toward the fulfillment of the expectations that belong to the essence of the Covenant.

Three events belong to the fortieth day: the "purification" of Mary, the "redemption" of the first-born child Jesus through an offering prescribed by the law, and the "presentation" of Jesus in the Temple.

In the infancy narrative overall, not least in this passage, it is easy to recognize the Jewish Christian substratum which is derived from the tradition of Jesus' family. But it has evidently been reformulated by a redactor who wrote and thought in Greek, and this person may reasonably be identified as the evangelist Luke himself. In this redaction, it is clear on the one hand that the writer lacked precise knowledge of Old Testament legislation, and on the other hand that his interest lay not in such details, but rather in the theological kernel of the event, which he wanted to make clear to his readers.

In the Book of Leviticus it is laid down that, after giving birth to a male child, a woman is impure for seven days (that is, she is excluded from taking part in worship), that the boy is to be circumcised on the eighth day, and that the woman must then remain at home a further thirty-three days for her blood to be purified (cf. *Lev* 12:1–4). After this she is to present a purification sacrifice: a lamb for a burnt-offering and a young pigeon or turtle-dove for a sin-offering. Poor people need bring only two turtle-doves or two young pigeons.

Mary presented the offering of the poor (cf. *Lk* 2:24). Luke, whose entire Gospel is shot through with a theology of the poor and a theology of poverty, is once again making it abundantly clear that Jesus' family belonged to the poor of Israel, and that it was among such as them that the promises would be fulfilled. Here too, we discover afresh what is meant by "under the law," what is meant when Jesus says to

John the Baptist that all righteousness must be fulfilled (cf. *Mt* 3:15). Mary does not need to be purified from the birth of Jesus: his birth ushers in the purification of the world. But she obeys the law, and in this way she serves the fulfillment of the promises.

The second event involved here is the redemption of the first-born, who belongs unreservedly to God. The price of the redemption was five shekels, and one could pay it to any priest one chose throughout the land.

Luke begins by specifically quoting the law regarding the consecration of the first-born: "Every male that opens the womb shall be called holy to the Lord" (2:23; cf. *Ex* 13:2; 13:12f., 15). What is unusual about this account is that instead of then relating the redemption of Jesus, it speaks of a third event: Jesus' presentation. Evidently Luke intends to say that instead of being "redeemed" and restored to his parents, this child was personally handed over to God in the Temple, given over completely to God. The verb *paristánai*, here translated as "to present," also means "to offer," in the way that sacrifices in the Temple were "offered." The language of sacrificial offering and priesthood is evoked here.

Luke has nothing to say regarding the act of "redemption" prescribed by the law. In its place we find the exact opposite: the child is handed over to God, and from now on belongs to him completely. None of the aforementioned acts prescribed by the law required an appearance in the Temple. Yet for Luke, Jesus' first entry into the Temple as the locus of the event is essential. Here, in the place of encounter between God and his people, instead of the reclamation of the first-born, what happens is that Jesus is publicly handed over to God, his Father.

This act—in the deepest sense of the word, a cultic act—is followed in Luke's Gospel by a scene of prophecy. The old man Simeon and the prophetess Anna, prompted by the Spirit of God, appear in the Temple, and as representatives of faithful Israel they greet the "Lord's Christ" (2:26).

Three things are said to us regarding Simeon: he is righteous (just), he is devout, and he is looking for the consolation of Israel. When we were considering the figure of Saint Joseph, we saw what a just man is: one whose life is lived in and from the word of God, in the will of God as expressed in the Torah. Simeon is "devout"—his whole person is oriented toward God. He is inwardly close to the Temple, he lives the encounter with God and awaits the "consolation of Israel." He lives for the Redeemer, for the one who is to come.

In the word "consolation" (paráklēsis), we hear echoes of the Johannine name for the Holy Spirit—the Paraclete, the consoling God. Simeon is a man of hope and expectation, and in this sense he already has the Holy Spirit upon him. We could say that he is a spiritual man and is therefore attuned to God's call, to his presence. So on this occasion he speaks as a prophet. First he takes the child Jesus into his arms and praises God, saying: "At last, all-powerful Master, you give leave to your servant to go in peace, according to your promise . . ." (*Lk* 2:29).

The form of the text, as presented by Luke, is already liturgical. In the churches of East and West it has formed part of the Church's night prayer from the earliest times. Together with the *Benedictus* and the *Magnificat*, which also come from Luke's infancy narratives, it belongs to the patrimony of prayer of the early Jewish Christian Church, into whose spirit-filled liturgical life we are here granted a privileged insight. In this prayer addressed to God, the child Jesus is spoken of as "your salvation," echoing the word *sōtēr* (Redeemer, Saviour) that we encountered in the angel's message on the Holy Night.

This canticle contains two Christological statements: Jesus is "the light to enlighten the Gentiles," and he gives "glory to your people Israel" (*Lk* 2:32). Both expressions are taken from the prophet Isaiah. The reference to the "light to enlighten the Gentiles" comes from the first and second Suffering Servant songs (cf. *Is* 42:6; 49:6). Jesus is identified as Isaiah's Suffering Servant—a mysterious figure, pointing toward the future. Central to the Servant's mission is universality, revelation to the Gentiles, to whom he brings God's light. The text referring to the glory of Israel is found in the prophet's words of consolation to suffering Israel, for whom help is promised through God's saving power (cf. *Is* 46:13).

Having given praise to God with the child in his arms, Simeon turns to Mary with a prophetic saying. After the joyful words spoken over the child, what he tells her is a kind of Passion prophecy (cf. *Lk* 2:34f.). Jesus is "set for the fall and rising of many in Israel," for a sign of contradiction. Simeon concludes with a very personal prophecy to the child's mother: "a sword will pierce through your own soul." The theology of glory is inseparably linked with the theology of the Cross. The Suffering Servant has the great mission to bring God's light to the world. Yet it is in the darkness of the Cross that this mission is fulfilled.

Beneath the language about the falling and rising of many, there are echoes of a prophecy from *Is* 8:14, in which God himself is designated as a rock against which men stumble and fall. So within the Passion saying, we see the deep bond that links Jesus with God himself. God and his word—Jesus, God's living word—are "signs," challenging us to make a choice. Man's "contradiction" of God runs all the way through history. What proves Jesus to be the true sign of God is that he takes upon himself the contradiction of God, he draws it to himself all the way to the contradiction of the Cross.

We are not talking about the past here. We all know to what extent Christ remains a sign of contradiction today, a contradiction that in the final analysis is directed at God. God himself is constantly regarded as a limitation placed on our freedom, that must be set aside if man is ever to be completely himself. God, with his truth, stands in opposition to man's manifold lies, his self-seeking and his pride.

God is love. But love can also be hated when it challenges us to transcend ourselves. It is not a romantic "good feeling." Redemption is not "wellness," it is not about basking in self-indulgence; on the contrary it is a liberation from imprisonment in self-absorption. This liberation comes at a price: the anguish of the Cross. The prophecy of light and that of the Cross belong together.

Finally, as we have seen, Simeon's Passion prophecy becomes quite specific—in the words spoken directly to Mary: "a sword will pierce through your own soul" (*Lk* 2:35). We may assume that this saying was preserved in the early Jewish Christian community as a personal recollection of Mary herself. The community would also have known, from the same source, what the saying had actually meant in practice. But we too can know this, in union with the believing and praying Church. The contradiction against the Son is also directed against the mother and it cuts her to the heart. For her, the Cross of radical contradiction becomes the sword that pierces through her soul. From Mary we can learn what true com-passion is: quite unsentimentally assuming the sufferings of others as one's own.

In the writings of the Church Fathers, a lack of feeling—insensitivity toward the suffering of others—is considered typical of paganism. In contrast to this attitude, the Christian faith holds up the God who suffers with men, and thereby draws us into his "com-passion." The *Mater Dolorosa*, the mother whose heart is pierced by a sword, is an iconic image of this fundamental attitude of Christian faith.

Alongside the prophet Simeon, there now appears the prophetess Anna, an 84-year-old woman, who after seven years of marriage, had lived for decades as a widow. "She did not depart from the Temple, worshipping with fasting and prayer night and day" (*Lk* 2:37). She is the model of the truly devout person. She is quite simply at home in the Temple. She lives with God and for God, body and soul. So she is truly a spirit-filled woman, a prophetess. Because she spends her life in the Temple—in adoration—she is there at the hour of Jesus' appearing. "Coming up at that very hour she gave thanks to God, and spoke of him to all who were looking for the redemption of Jerusalem" (*Lk* 2:38). Her prophecy consists in her proclamation—in passing on to others the hope by which she lives.

. . .

Luke concludes his account of Jesus' birth, which included the implementation of all the requirements of the law (cf. 2:39), by announcing the return of the Holy Family to Nazareth. "The child grew and became strong, filled with wisdom; and the favor of God was upon him" (2:40).

CHAPTER IV

The Wise Men from the East and the Flight into Egypt

THE HISTORICAL AND GEOGRAPHICAL FRAMEWORK OF THE NARRATIVE

Hardly any biblical narrative has so caught the imagination or stimulated so much research and reflection as the account of the "Magi" from the "land of the sunrise," which the evangelist Matthew adds directly after the story of Jesus' birth: "Now when Jesus was born in Bethlehem of Judea in the days of Herod the king, behold, wise men from the East came to Jerusalem, saying, 'Where is he who has been born king of the Jews? For we have seen his star in the East, and have come to worship him'" (*Mt* 2:1f.).

To begin with, Matthew clearly establishes the historical setting by the references to King Herod and to Bethlehem as the place of birth. A historical figure and a known geographical location are named. Yet these factual details already include elements of interpretation. Rudolf Pesch in his short book *Die matthäischen Weihnachtsgeschichten* highlights the theological significance of the figure of Herod: "Just as the Christmas Gospel (*Lk* 2:1–21) begins by naming the Roman Emperor Augustus, so the narrative in *Mt* 2 begins by naming the 'king of the Jews', Herod. If in the former case, the Emperor, with his claim to have brought peace to the world, is the total antithesis of the newborn child, so too is the king who reigns by the Emperor's favor—with his quasi-Messianic claim to be the redeemer at least of the Jewish kingdom" (pp. 23f.).

Bethlehem is the birthplace of King David. In the course of the narrative, further light will be shed on the theological significance of this place through the answer given by the scribes to Herod's question where the Messiah would be born. Matthew's addition of the qualifying phrase "of Judea" to the geographical location of Bethlehem could suggest a subsidiary theological theme. In the context of Jacob's blessing, the patriarch prophesies to his son Judah: "The sceptre shall not depart from Judah nor the ruler's staff from between his feet, until he comes to whom it belongs, and to him shall be the obedience of the peoples" (*Gen* 49:10). In a narrative concerned with the coming of the definitive

David—the newborn king of the Jews who is to redeem all peoples—there are echoes of this prophecy in the background.

Another passage to be read alongside Jacob's blessing is a saying attributed in the Bible to the pagan prophet Balaam. Balaam is a historical figure, for whom there is extrabiblical confirmation. In 1967, on the East Bank of the Jordan, an inscription was discovered in which Balaam, son of Beor, is named as a "seer" of autochthonous deities: various oracles, both of doom and salvation, are ascribed to him (cf. Hans-Peter Müller, *"Bileam"*). The Bible presents him as a soothsayer in the service of the king of Moab, who asks him to curse Israel. Balaam intends to do so, but God himself intervenes, causing the prophet to proclaim a blessing upon Israel instead of a curse. In the biblical tradition he is nevertheless dismissed as an agitator for idolatry and executed (cf. *Num* 31:8; *Jos* 13:22). All the more important, then, is the saving prophecy ascribed to him, a non-Jew and a worshipper of other gods, and it is a prophecy that was evidently known outside Israel: "I see him, but not now; I behold him, but not nigh: a star shall come forth out of Jacob and a sceptre shall rise out of Israel" (*Num* 24:17).

It is surprising that Matthew, who is usually so eager to present events in the life and ministry of Jesus as the fulfillment of Old Testament prophecies, does not actually quote this text, which features prominently in the history of the exegesis of the Magi story. It is true that Balaam's star is not a celestial body: the coming king is himself the star that shines upon the world and determines its fate. Still, the context of star and kingship could have influenced the idea of a star that pertains to *this* king and points toward him.

Hence we may freely assume that this non-Jewish, "pagan" oracle would have circulated outside Judaism in some shape or form and would have set people thinking. The question how people outside Israel were able to recognize in a "king of the Jews" the bearer of a salvation destined also for them, is one to which we will return.

WHO WERE THE "MAGI"?

First, though, we have to ask what sort of people they were, these "Magi" from the "land of sunrise," as Matthew calls them. In the relevant sources, the concept of Magi (*mágoi*) encompasses a wide range of meanings, from the wholly positive to the wholly negative.

According to the first of the four principal meanings, Magi are understood to be members of the Persian priestly caste. In Hellenistic culture they were regarded as "rulers of a distinctive religion," but at the same time their religious ideas were thought to be "strongly influenced by philosophy," so that the Greek philosophers have often been portrayed as their pupils (cf. Delling, "*mágos*," p. 356). No doubt this view contains some not easily definable element of truth: after all, Aristotle himself spoke of the philosophical work of the Magi (cf. *ibid.*, p. 357).

The other meanings listed by Gerhard Delling are as follows: possessors and users of supernatural knowledge and ability, magicians, and finally deceivers and seducers. In the Acts of the Apostles we find an example of this final meaning: a Magus named Bar-Jesus is described by Paul as "son of the devil, enemy of all righteousness" (13:10) and he suffers a corresponding fate.

The ambivalence of the concept of Magi that we find here illustrates the ambivalence of religion in general. It can become the path to true knowledge, the path to Jesus Christ. But when it fails, in his presence, to open up to him and actually opposes the one God and Saviour, it becomes demonic and destructive.

In the New Testament, then, we encounter two contrasting types of "Magi": in Saint Matthew's Magi story, religious and philosophical wisdom is obviously an incentive to set off in the right direction, it is the wisdom that ultimately leads people to Christ. In the Acts of the Apostles, though, we find the other type of Magus: one who pits his own power against the messenger of Jesus Christ and thereby sides with the demons, even though Jesus has already defeated them.

. . .

Clearly, for the Magi in *Mt* 2, it is the first of the four meanings that applies, at least in a broad sense. Even if they were not exactly members of the Persian priesthood, they were nevertheless custodians of religious and philosophical knowledge that had developed in that area and continued to be cultivated there.

Naturally, attempts have been made to establish more precisely who they were. The Viennese astronomer Konradin Ferrari d'Occhieppo has shown that in the city of Babylon—which had once been a center of scientific astronomy but was already in decline by the time of Jesus—there was still "a small group of astronomers who were gradually dying out . . . Earthenware tablets, covered in cuneiform signs with astronomical calculations . . . are clear proof of this" (*Der Stern von Bethlehem*, p. 27). He goes on to say that the conjunction of the planets Jupiter and Saturn in the constellation Pisces in the years 7–6 B.C.—now believed to be the actual time of Jesus' birth—is something that the Babylonian astronomers could have calculated, and it may well have pointed them toward the land of Judea and to a newborn "king of the Jews."

We will come back to the question of the star at a later stage. For the time being, we should ask what sort of people they were, who set out on the path to the king. They could have been astronomers; but not everyone who could predict and observe the conjunction of the planets would have associated this with a king in Judea who held some significance for them. Before the star could convey a message, there had to be a promise in circulation, something akin to Balaam's oracle. We know from Tacitus and Suetonius that speculation was rife at the time that the ruler of the world would emerge from Judah—an expectation that Flavius Josephus applied to Vespasian, consequently finding his way into the latter's favor (cf. *De Bello Judaico* iii, 399–408).

All kinds of factors could have combined to generate the idea that the language of the star contained a message of hope. But none of this would have prompted people to set off on a journey, unless they were people of inner unrest, people of hope, people on the lookout for the true star of salvation. The men of whom Matthew speaks were not just astronomers. There were "wise." They represent the inner dynamic of religion toward self-transcendence, which involves a search for truth, a search for the true God and hence "philosophy" in the original sense of the word. Wisdom, then, serves to purify the message of "science": the rationality of that message does not remain at the level of intellectual knowledge, but seeks understanding in its fullness, and so raises reason to its loftiest possibilities.

From all that has been said, we can obtain some sense of the outlook and the knowledge that prompted these men to set off in search of the newborn "king of the Jews." We could well say that they represent the religions moving toward Christ, as well as the self-transcendence of science toward him. In a way they are the successors of Abraham, who set off on a journey in response to God's call. In another way they are the successors of Socrates and his habit of questioning above and beyond conventional religion toward the higher truth. In this sense, these figures are forerunners, preparers of the way, seekers after truth, such as we find in every age.

Just as the Church's tradition read the Christmas story quite spontaneously in the light of *Is* 1:3, with the result that the ox and the ass found their way into the crib, so too the Magi story was read in conjunction with *Ps* 72:10 and *Is* 60. Hence the wise men from the East became kings, and with them camels and dromedaries were added to the crib.

While the prophetic content of these texts expands the provenance of these figures to include the extreme west (Tarshish = Tartessos in Spain), tradition has further developed this idea of universality by conceiving them as kings from all three known continents: Africa, Asia, and Europe. The black king is part and parcel of this: in the kingdom of Jesus Christ there are no distinctions of race and origin. In him and through him, humanity is united, yet without losing any of the richness of variety.

Later, the three kings came to be associated with the phases of human life—youth, maturity, and old age. This too makes good sense, highlighting the fact that each of the various stages of human life finds its true meaning and its inner unity in companionship with Jesus.

The key point is this: the wise men from the east are a new beginning. They represent the journeying of humanity toward Christ. They initiate a procession that continues throughout history. Not only do they represent the people who have found the way to Christ: they represent the inner aspiration of the human spirit, the dynamism of religions and human reason toward him.

THE STAR

Now we must come back to the star which showed the wise men their path, as we read in Saint Matthew's account. What kind of star was it? Was there a star at all?

Distinguished exegetes like Rudolf Pesch take the view that this is not a sensible question to ask. We are dealing with a theological narrative that should not be confused with astronomy. A similar position was put forward in the early Church by Saint John Chrysostom: "That this star was not of the common sort, or rather not a star at all, as it seems at least to me, but some invisible power transformed into this appearance, is in the first place evident from its very course. For there is . . . not any star that moves by this way" (*In Matthaeum Homiliae*, VI, 2: PG 57, 64). Much of the Church's tradition has underlined the miraculous nature of the star, as in the writings of Ignatius of Antioch (c. 100 A.D.), who saw the sun and the moon dancing around the star, and likewise in the ancient Epiphany hymn from the Roman Breviary, which states that the star outshone the sun in beauty and brilliance.

Nevertheless, the question whether or not this was an astronomically identifiable and classifiable celestial apparition was not going to go away. It would be wrong to dismiss it *a priori* on account of the theological character of the story. With the emergence of modern astronomy, developed by believing Christians, the question of this star has been revisited.

Johannes Kepler († 1630) proposed a solution that in its key elements has been put forward again by astronomers today. Kepler calculated that in the year 7–6 B.C., which as we have seen is now thought likely to have been when Jesus was born, there was a conjunction of the planets Jupiter, Saturn and Mars. He himself had experienced a similar conjunction in the year 1604, with the further addition of a supernova. This is a weak or very distant star in which a colossal explosion takes place, so that for weeks and months an intensive radiance streams from it. Kepler regarded the supernova as a new star. He took the view that the planetary conjunction at the time of Jesus' birth must also have been accompanied by a supernova, and this was how he attempted to explain the phenomenon of the bright star of Bethlehem in astronomical terms. It is interesting, moreover, that the Göttingen scholar Friedrich Wieseler seems to have discovered a reference in Chinese chronological tables to the fact that in 4 B.C. "a bright star appeared and was visible for quite a long time" (Gnilka, *Das Matthäusevangelium*, p. 44).

The aforementioned astronomer Ferrari d'Occhieppo has dismissed the theory of the supernova. For him a sufficient explanation of the star of Bethlehem is provided by the conjunction of Jupiter and Saturn in the constellation Pisces, which he believed he could determine with chronological precision. It is important here to note that the planet Jupiter stood for the principal Babylonian god Marduk. Ferrari d'Occhieppo concludes as follows: "Jupiter, the star of the highest Babylonian deity, entered its brightest phase when it rose in the evening alongside Saturn, the cosmic representative of the Jewish people" (*Der Stern von Bethlehem*, p. 52). We need not go into the details. From this planetary encounter, according to Ferrari d'Occhieppo, Babylonian astronomers were able to conclude that there had been a universally significant event: the birth in the land of the Jews of a ruler who would bring salvation.

What are we to make of all this? The great conjunction of Jupiter and Saturn in the sign of Pisces in 7–6 B.C. seems to be an established fact. It could well have pointed astronomers from the Babylonian-Persian region toward the land of the Jews, toward a "king of the Jews." Exactly how those men came to the conviction that prompted them to set off and led them eventually to Jerusalem and Bethlehem, must remain an open question. The constellation could have set them thinking, it could have been the first signal for their outward and inward departure. But it would not have been able to speak to them, had they not already been moved in some other way, inwardly moved by the hope of the star that was to rise over Jacob (cf. *Num* 24:17).

If these wise men, led by the star to search for the king of the Jews, represent the movement of the Gentiles toward Christ, this implies that the cosmos speaks of Christ, even though its language is not yet fully intelligible to man in his present state. The language of creation provides a great many pointers. It gives man an intuition of the Creator. Moreover, it arouses the expectation, indeed the hope, that this God will one day reveal himself. And at the same time it elicits an awareness that man can and should approach him. But the knowledge that emerges from creation, and acquires concrete form in the religions, can also become disoriented, so that it no longer prompts man to transcend himself, but induces him to lock himself into systems with which he believes he can, in some way, oppose the hidden powers of the world.

In our story both elements can be seen: in the first instance, the star leads the wise men as far as Judea. It is quite natural that their search for the newborn king of the Jews should take them to Israel's royal city and to the king's palace. That, surely, is where the future king must have been born. Then they need the direction provided by Israel's sacred Scriptures—the words of the living God—in order to find the way once and for all to David's true heir.

The Fathers have emphasized a further aspect. Gregory Nazianzen says that at the very moment when the Magi adored Jesus, astrology came to an end, as the stars from then on traced the orbit determined by Christ (cf. *Poem. Dogm.* V 55–64: PG 37, 428–429). In the ancient world, the heavenly bodies were regarded as divine powers, determining men's fate. The planets bear the names of deities. According to the concept prevailing at the time, they somehow ruled over the world, and man had to try to appease these powers. Biblical monotheism soon brought about a clear demythologization: with marvelous sobriety, the creation account describes the sun and the moon—the great divinities of the pagan world—as lights that God placed in the sky alongside the entire firmament of stars (cf. *Gen* 1:16f.).

On entering the Gentile world, the Christian faith had to grapple once again with the question of the astral divinities. Hence in the letters he wrote from prison to the Ephesians and the Colossians, Paul emphasizes that the risen Christ has conquered all the powers and forces in the heavens, and that he reigns over the entire universe. The story of the wise men's star makes a similar point: it is not the star that determines the child's destiny, it is the child that directs the star.

If we wish, we may speak here of a kind of anthropological revolution: human nature assumed by God—as revealed in God's only-begotten Son—is greater than all the powers of the material world, greater than the entire universe.

JERUSALEM—STOPPING POINT ON THE JOURNEY

It is time to return to the text of the Gospel. The wise men have arrived at the king's palace in Jerusalem, which they presume must be the place of the promise. They inquire after the newborn "king of the Jews." This is a typically non-Jewish expression. In Jewish circles, people would speak of the "king of Israel." In fact, this "Gentile" title, "king of the Jews," does not reappear until Jesus' trial and the inscription over the Cross, in both cases used by the Gentile Pilate (cf. *Mk* 15:9; *Jn* 19:19–22). So we could say that here—as the first Gentiles inquire after Jesus—there are already echoes of the mystery of the Cross, a mystery that is inseparably linked with Jesus' kingship.

These echoes can be heard clearly in the reaction to the Magi's question about the newborn king: "Herod was troubled and all Jerusalem with him" (*Mt* 2:3). The exegetes point out that in Herod's case, it was quite understandable that he was troubled by this news of the birth of a mysterious pretender to the throne. Less understandable, though, is the fact that all Jerusalem seems to have been troubled as well. This element could be an anticipation of Jesus' regal entrance into the Holy City on the eve of his Passion, when Matthew says that the whole city was quaking (cf. *Mt* 21:10). In this way the two scenes, both in some way manifesting Jesus' kingship, are linked to one another and to the Passion theme.

It seems to me that the reference to the troubled state of the city at the time of the Magi's visit makes good sense. In order to clarify the question about the pretender to the throne, for him a highly dangerous question, Herod called together "all the chief priests and scribes of the people" (*Mt* 2:4). Such a gathering and its purpose could not have remained unknown. The supposed or actual birth of a Messianic king would inevitably bring trial and tribulation to the people of Jerusalem. They knew Herod, after all. What from the lofty perspective of faith is a star of hope, from the perspective of daily life is merely a disturbance, a cause for concern and fear. It is true: God disturbs our comfortable day-to-day existence. Jesus' kingship goes hand in hand with his Passion.

What answer did the illustrious assembly give to the question about Jesus' birthplace? According to *Mt* 2:6, the answer combined a passage from the prophet Micah with one from the Second Book of Samuel: "And you, O Bethlehem, in the land of Judah, are by no means least among the leading cities of Judah; for from you shall come a ruler (cf. *Mic* 5:1) who will govern my people Israel (cf. 2 *Sam* 5:2)."

Matthew has made two slight adjustments to the quoted text. Whereas the greater part of the textual tradition, particularly the Greek translation (LXX), says: "You are the smallest among the clans of Judah," he writes "You are by no means least among the leading cities of Judah." Both versions of the text, each in its own way, illustrate the paradoxical element in God's way of acting, which runs through the whole of the Old Testament: greatness emerges from what seems in earthly terms small and insignificant, while worldly greatness collapses and falls.

So it is, for example, in the account of the call of David. The youngest of Jesse's sons, who was busy looking after the sheep, has to be summoned and is anointed king: it is not outward appearance or height of stature that counts, but the heart (cf. 1 *Sam* 16:7). One of Mary's sayings from the *Magnificat* sums up this perennial paradox in God's action: "He has put down the mighty from their thrones, and exalted those of low degree" (*Lk* 1:52). The version of the Old Testament text that describes Bethlehem as small among the clans of Judah, clearly expresses this divine *modus operandi*.

Yet when Matthew writes: "You are by no means least among the leading cities of Judah," he only appears to resolve the paradox. This small city, considered insignificant in itself, can now be recognized in its true greatness. Out of her comes the true shepherd of Israel: human estimation and divine response are combined in this version of the text. In Jesus' birth in a cave outside the city, the paradox is once again confirmed.

So now we come to the second adjustment: Matthew has added to the prophetic text the aforementioned phrase from the Second Book of Samuel (5:2), originally applied to the new King David, and now brought to fulfillment in Jesus. The coming ruler is portrayed as the shepherd of Israel. In this way, Matthew highlights the loving care and tenderness that mark out the true ruler as a representative of God's kingship.

The answer given by the chief priests and scribes to the wise men's question has a thoroughly practical geographical content, which helps the Magi on their way. Yet it is not only a geographical, but also a theological interpretation of the place and the event. That Herod would draw the obvious conclusion is understandable. Yet it is remarkable that his Scripture experts do not feel prompted to take any practical steps as a result. Does this, perhaps, furnish us with the image of a theology that exhausts itself in academic disputes?

THE WORSHIP OF THE WISE MEN BEFORE JESUS

The star had evidently receded from view in Jerusalem. After their encounter with the words of Scripture, it shone for the wise men once more. Creation, interpreted by the Scriptures, speaks to humanity again. In describing the wise men's reaction, Matthew reaches for superlatives: "When they saw the star, they rejoiced exceedingly with great joy" (2:10). It is the joy of one whose heart has received a ray of God's light and who can now see that his hope has been realized—the joy of one who has found what he sought, and has himself been found.

"Going into the house they saw the child with Mary his mother, and they fell down and worshipped him" (*Mt* 2:11). Strikingly absent from this sentence is any mention of Saint Joseph, even though Matthew's infancy narrative was written from Joseph's perspective. We meet only "Mary, his mother" by the side of Jesus at the scene of adoration. I have yet to find a completely convincing explanation. There are one or two passages in the Old Testament where particular significance is attached to the figure of the queen mother (e.g. *Jer* 13:18). But this is probably not enough. No doubt Gnilka is correct when he suggests that this is Matthew's way of reminding us of the virgin birth and marking Jesus out as the Son of God (cf. *Das Matthäusevangelium*, p. 40).

The wise men do a *proskýnesis* before the royal child, that is to say they throw themselves onto the ground before him. This is the homage that is offered to a divine king. The gifts brought by the wise men may be explained in similar terms. They are not practical gifts, of a kind that the holy family might have had a use for at this moment. They express the same thing as the *proskýnesis*: they acknowledge the royal dignity of him to whom they are offered. Gold and incense are also mentioned in *Is* 60:6 as gifts of homage that the Gentiles will place before the God of Israel.

In the Church's tradition—with certain variations—the three gifts have been thought to represent three aspects of the mystery of Christ: the gold points to Jesus' kingship, the incense to his divine sonship, the myrrh to the mystery of his Passion.

The myrrh actually appears in Saint John's Gospel after the death of Jesus: John tells us that Nicodemus had prepared myrrh, among other ointments, for the anointing of Jesus' body (cf. *Jn* 19:39). Through the myrrh, then, the mystery of the Cross is once again associated with Jesus' kingship and mysteriously proclaimed in the worship offered by the wise men. Anointing is an attempt to resist death, which only becomes definitive with decomposition. By the time the women came to the tomb to anoint the body on Easter morning—a task that could not be carried out on the evening of the crucifixion because of the approaching feast-day—Jesus had already risen. He no longer needed myrrh as a protection against death, because God's life itself had overcome death.

Flight into Egypt and return
to the Land of Israel

After the end of the Magi story, Saint Joseph reappears as the principal actor on the stage, albeit acting not on his own initiative but in accordance with instructions that he receives once more from the angel of God in a dream. He is asked to rise in haste and take the child and its mother, to flee to Egypt, and to remain there pending further instructions, "for Herod is about to search for the child, to destroy him" (*Mt* 2:13).

In 7 B.C. Herod had had his sons Alexander and Aristobulus executed, as he considered them a threat to his power. In 4 B.C. he killed his son Antipater for the same reason (cf. Stuhlmacher, *Die Geburt des Immanuel*, p. 85). He thought solely in terms of power. The news the wise men brought him of a pretender to the throne must have alarmed him. It was clear from his character that he would stop at nothing.

"Then Herod, when he saw that he had been tricked by the wise men, was in a furious rage, and he sent and killed all the male children in Bethlehem and in all that region who were two years old or under, according to the time which he had ascertained from the wise men" (*Mt* 2:16). It is true that we have no record of this event from non-biblical sources, yet in view of all the atrocities that Herod did commit, that is not enough to prove that it did not take place. Rudolf Pesch quotes the Jewish author Abraham Schalit on the subject:

"Belief in the proximate arrival or birth of the Messianic king was in the air at the time. The suspicious tyrant sensed betrayal and hostility everywhere, and a vague rumour reaching his ears would have been enough to put into his sick mind the idea of killing the newborn children. There is nothing impossible about this command" (*Die matthäischen Weihnachtsgeschichten*, p. 72).

The historicity of the event is admittedly questioned by a number of exegetes on the basis of a further consideration: what we encounter here is the widespread motif of the persecuted child-king, one that contemporary literature applied to Moses in a form that could have served as a model for this story about Jesus. It must be said, though, that most of the examples cited fail to convince, and most of them are later than Matthew's Gospel. The closest to it in date and content is the *Moses Haggadah* handed down by Flavius Josephus, which gives a new twist to the biblical story of the birth and rescue of Moses.

The Book of Exodus relates that, as the Jewish population grew in numbers and significance, Pharaoh sensed a threat to his land of Egypt, and so he not only persecuted the Jewish minority through forced labor, but he gave orders that their newborn male children were to be killed. Moses was rescued through a ruse of his mother and he grew up at the Egyptian court as an adopted son of Pharaoh's daughter;

later, though, he had to flee on account of his support for the tormented Jewish population (cf. *Ex* 2).

The *Moses Haggadah* tells the story differently: learned men had prophesied to the king that a boy would be born of Hebrew blood around that time, who in later life would put an end to Egyptian domination and make the Israelites powerful. At this, the king ordered that all Hebrew boys be thrown into the river and killed at birth. But God appeared in a dream to Moses' father and promised to save the child (cf. Gnilka, *Das Matthäusevangelium*, p. 34f.). Here, the slaughter of the Jewish boys takes place not for the reason given in the Book of Exodus, but in order to make sure that the promised leader, Moses, is eliminated.

Both the motive for the killings and the father's vision in a dream, with a promise of rescue, bring this story close to that of Jesus, Herod and the slaughtered innocents. But these similarities are not enough to make Matthew's account look like a mere Christian variation on the theme of the *Moses Haggadah*. The differences between the two narratives are too great. What is more, the *Antiquitates* of Flavius Josephus are almost certainly *later* in date than Matthew's Gospel, even if the story itself probably belongs to an older tradition.

With a rather different end in view, Matthew himself alludes to the Moses story, hoping to find there the interpretation of the whole event. He sees the key to understanding in the prophecy: "Out of Egypt I called my son" (*Hos* 11:1). Hosea portrays the history of Israel as a love story between God and his people. In this passage, though, God's favor toward Israel is presented not through the image of conjugal love, but that of parental love: "Hence Israel receives the further title 'son' . . . in the sense of an adoptive sonship. The fundamental act of paternal love is the son's liberation from Egypt" (Deissler, *Zwölf Propheten*, p. 50). For Matthew, the prophet is speaking here of Christ—the *true* son. It is he whom the Father loves and calls out of Egypt.

For the evangelist, the history of Israel begins afresh when Jesus returns from Egypt to the Holy Land. Israel's first homecoming from the land of slavery had in many respects been a failure. Hosea tells us that in response to the father's call, the "son" ran away: "The more I called them, the more they went from me" (11:2). This running away from the call to liberation leads to a new form of slavery: "They shall return to the land of Egypt and Assyria shall be their king because they have refused to return to me" (11:5). Thus Israel constantly finds itself back in Egypt, as it were.

With the flight into Egypt and the return to the promised land, Jesus grants the definitive Exodus. He is truly the Son. He is not going to run away from the Father. He returns home, and he leads others home. He is always on the path toward God and thus he leads the way back from exile to the homeland, back to all that is authentic and true. Jesus, the true Son, himself went into "exile" in a very deep sense, in order to lead all of us home from exile.

Matthew ends his short account of the slaughter of the innocents, which follows the flight into Egypt, with another prophetic text, this time taken from Jeremiah: "A voice is heard in Ramah, lamentation and bitter weeping. Rachel is weeping for her children; she refuses to be comforted for her children, because they are not" (31:15; cf. *Mt* 2:18). Jeremiah situates these words in the context of a prophecy filled with hope and joy, in which the prophet confidently announces the restoration of Israel: "He who scattered Israel will gather him, and will keep him as a shepherd keeps his flock. For the Lord has ransomed Jacob, and has redeemed him from hands too strong for him" (31:10f.).

The entire chapter probably dates from the early period of Jeremiah's work, when on the one hand the decline of the Assyrian Empire and on the other the cultic reforms of King Josiah had revived hopes for a restoration of the northern kingdom of Israel—a territory populated largely by the tribes of Joseph and Benjamin, the children of Rachel. In Jeremiah's text, then, immediately after the lament of the mother of those tribes, there is a word of consolation: "Thus says the Lord: 'Keep your voice from weeping, and your eyes from tears; for your work shall be rewarded, says the Lord, and they shall come back from the land of the enemy'" (31:16).

In Matthew, we find two changes vis-à-vis the prophet: in Jeremiah's day, Rachel's tomb was situated on the Benjaminite-Ephraimite border, that is, on the border of the northern kingdom, the tribal territory of Rachel's sons—not far, as it happens, from the home of the prophet. Still during Old Testament times, the tomb was moved south, to the Bethlehem area, and that is where it was for Matthew.

The second change is that the evangelist omits the consoling promise of a return home: only the lament is quoted, the mother remains unconsoled. So in Matthew's version, the prophetic text—the mother's lament without the consoling response—is like a cry to God himself, a plea for consolation that does not come and is still awaited, a plea to which only God can respond. For the only true consolation that is more than mere words would be the resurrection. Only in the resurrection could the wrong be overcome, and that bitter lament "they are not" be silenced. In our own day, the mothers' cry to God continues unabated, yet at the same time the resurrection of Jesus strengthens our hope of true consolation.

The concluding section of Matthew's infancy narrative ends with a further proof-text, intended to unlock the meaning of the entire event. Once again the figure of Saint Joseph looms large. Twice he receives instructions in a dream, and thus he is presented to us once again as the listening and discerning one, the obedient one who is also decisive and acts wisely. At first he is told that Herod has died and that the time has therefore come for him and his family to return home. The return journey is presented with a certain solemnity: "He went to the land of Israel" (2:21).

Straight away he is caught up in the tragic situation that afflicted Israel at that stage in its history: he learns that Archelaus, the most brutal of Herod's sons, is ruling Judea. So it cannot be there—that is to say in Bethlehem—that the family of Jesus is to live. Joseph is now instructed, in a dream, to go to Galilee.

The fact that Joseph, on becoming aware of the problems in Judea, did not simply continue on his own initiative into Galilee to live under the less brutal regime of Antipas, but was instructed by the angel to go there, is intended to show that Jesus' Galilean origin corresponds to God's design for history. In Jesus' public ministry, any reference to his Galilean origin was always seen as a proof that he could not be the promised Messiah. Matthew almost imperceptibly rebuts this argument here. Shortly afterward, at the beginning of Jesus' public ministry, he returns to the theme and argues, on the basis of *Is* 8:23–9:2, that the place where the "great light" is to rise is where the "land of darkness" is—the former northern kingdom, the "land of Zebulun and the land of Naphtali" (cf. *Mt* 4:14–16).

Yet Matthew has to respond to an even more concrete objection, namely that no mention is made of Nazareth in any of the promises: surely the Saviour could not come from there (cf. *Jn* 1:46). To this the evangelist responds: "Joseph went and dwelt in a city called Nazareth, that what was spoken by the prophets might be fulfilled, 'He shall be called a Nazarene'" (*Mt* 2:23). By this he means: the label "Nazarene," applied to Jesus with reference to his place of origin—already an established fact by the time the Gospel was written down—reveals that he is indeed the heir to the promise. Here, in contrast to the earlier proof-texts, Matthew is not referring to any particular Scriptural passage, but to the prophets overall. Their hope is summed up in this designation of Jesus.

In this verse, Matthew presents exegetes of every era with a difficult problem: where among the prophets is the source for this word of hope to be found?

Before we examine this question, a few linguistic observations may be helpful. The New Testament uses the two labels *Nazōraios* and *Nazarēnos* in reference to Jesus. *Nazōraios* is used in Matthew, John and the Acts of the Apostles, *Nazarēnos* is used in Mark; Luke's Gospel has both forms. In the Semitic linguistic world, Jesus' disciples were known as *Nazōraioi*, whereas in the Graeco-Roman world they were called Christians (cf. *Acts* 11:26). So now we must ask quite specifically: is there any trace in the Old Testament of a promise linked to the word *Nazōraios* that could be applied to Jesus?

Ansgar Wucherpfennig in his monograph on Saint Joseph has carefully summarized the difficult exegetical debate. I will attempt to draw out only the most important elements. There are two principal approaches toward a solution.

The first is based on the prophecy of the birth of the judge Samson. Of him, the angel who announces his birth says that he will be a "Nazirite," consecrated to God from his mother's womb "to the day of his death," as his mother recounts (cf. *Judg* 13:5–7). One argument against this suggested etymology of the label *Nazōraios* as applied to Jesus is that he did not fulfill the criteria of a Nazirite that are given in the Book of Judges, especially the alcohol prohibition. He was no Nazirite in the classical sense of the term. Nevertheless, it could be said of him, in a manner far surpassing such external details, that he was totally consecrated to God, completely made over to God, from his mother's womb to the day of his death. If we recall what Luke says about the presentation of Jesus—"the first-born"—to God in the Temple, and if we keep before our eyes the way John's Gospel portrays Jesus as the one who comes completely from the Father, lives wholly from him and for him, then we see with extraordinary clarity that Jesus was indeed consecrated to God, from his mother's womb until his death on the Cross.

The second approach sets out from the idea that at the root of the name *Nazōraios* one may detect the Hebrew word *nezer*, which is found at the heart of the prophecy of *Is* 11:1: "There shall come forth a shoot (*nezer*) from the stump of Jesse." This prophetic saying has to be read in the context of the Messianic trilogy formed by *Is* 7 ("a virgin shall conceive"), *Is* 9 (light in the darkness, "unto us a child is born") and *Is* 11 (the shoot from the stump, over whom the Spirit of the Lord rests). Since Matthew refers explicitly to *Is* 7 and *Is* 9, it makes sense to assume a reference in his text to *Is* 11 as well. The unusual element in this promise is that it extends back beyond David to Jesse, the father of the tribe. From the stump that seemed already dead, God brings forth a new shoot: he launches a new beginning, albeit one that remains in profound continuity with the earlier history of the promises.

How could one fail to be reminded here of the ending of Matthew's genealogy, which on the one hand is steeped in the utter continuity of God's saving action, and yet breaks off at the end and speaks of an entirely new beginning, as God himself intervenes and brings about a birth that is no longer the fruit of human "begetting"? Indeed, we have good reason to suppose that Matthew detected in the name of Nazareth a prophetic reference to the "shoot" (*nezer*), and that he saw the use of the designation *Nazōraios* for Jesus as a sign of the fulfillment of God's promise to draw new life from the dead stump of Jesse, upon whom the Spirit of God would rest.

If we add that in the inscription above the Cross, Jesus

is called *ho Nazōraios* (cf. *Jn* 19:19), then the title acquires its full resonance: what at first sight refers simply to his origin, actually points to his essence: he is the "shoot," he is the one completely consecrated to God, from his mother's womb to the day of his death.

At the end of this lengthy chapter, the question arises: how are we to understand all this? Are we dealing with history that actually took place, or is it merely a theological meditation, presented under the guise of stories? In this regard, Jean Daniélou rightly observes: "The adoration of the Magi, unlike the story of the annunciation [to Mary], does not touch upon any essential aspect of our faith. No foundations would be shaken if it were simply an invention of Matthew's based on a theological idea" (*The Infancy Narratives*, p. 95). Daniélou himself, though, comes to the conclusion that we are dealing here with historical events, whose theological significance was worked out by the Jewish Christian community and by Matthew.

To put it simply, I share this view. In any case, it should be noted that over the last fifty years there has been an about-turn in thinking on this question of historicity, based not on new historical knowledge, but rather on a changed attitude to sacred Scripture and to the Christian message in general. While Gerhard Delling in the fourth volume of the *Theological Dictionary of the New Testament* (1942) was still convinced of the historicity of the Magi story on the basis of historical research (cf. p. 358, n. 11), since that time, even exegetes as ecclesially minded as Ernst Nellessen and Rudolf Pesch have rejected historicity, or at least they have left the question open.

An interesting comment, in the light of this situation, is the carefully argued position presented by Klaus Berger in his 2011 commentary on the whole of the New Testament: "Even when there is only a single attestation . . . one must suppose, until the contrary is proven, that the evangelists did not intend to deceive their readers, but rather to inform them concerning historical events . . . to contest the historicity of this account on mere suspicion exceeds every imaginable competence of historians" (*Kommentar zum Neuen Testament*, p. 20).

With this view I can only agree. The two chapters of Matthew's Gospel devoted to the infancy narratives are not a meditation presented under the guise of stories, but the converse: Matthew is recounting real history, theologically thought through and interpreted, and thus he helps us to understand the mystery of Jesus more deeply.

The Twelve-Year-Old Jesus in the Temple

Besides the story of Jesus' birth, Saint Luke has preserved for us one further small and precious element of tradition regarding our Lord's childhood, in which the mystery of Jesus is illuminated in a very particular way. It is recounted that Jesus' parents went on pilgrimage every year to Jerusalem for the Feast of the Passover. Jesus' family was devout: they observed the law.

In some portrayals of the figure of Jesus, the emphasis is placed almost exclusively on the radical aspects, on Jesus' challenge to false piety. Thus Jesus is presented as a liberal or a revolutionary. It is true that in his mission as Son, Jesus did introduce a new phase in man's relationship to God, opening up a new dimension of human intimacy with God. But this was not an attack on Israel's piety. Jesus' freedom is not the freedom of the liberal. It is the freedom of the Son, and thus the freedom of the truly devout person. As Son, Jesus brings a new freedom: not the freedom of someone with no obligations, but the freedom of someone totally united with the Father's will, someone who helps mankind to attain the freedom of inner oneness with God.

Jesus came not to abolish, but to complete (cf. *Mt* 5:17). This link between radical newness and equally radical faithfulness, rooted in Jesus' sonship, emerges clearly in the short narrative about the twelve-year-old: indeed, I would say it is the actual theological content that this story is intended to convey.

Let us return to Jesus' parents. The Torah laid down that every Israelite was to make an appearance in the Temple for the three great feasts—Passover, Feast of Weeks (Pentecost) and Feast of Tabernacles (cf. *Ex* 23:17; 34:23f.; *Deut* 16:16f.). The question whether women were also obliged to make this pilgrimage was a matter of debate between the schools of Shammai and Hillel. As for boys, the obligation applied to them once they had completed their thirteenth year. But it is also laid down that they were to accustom themselves gradually to the commandments. One way of doing this was to make the pilgrimage at the age of twelve. The fact that Mary and Jesus also took part in the pilgrimage once again demonstrates the piety of Jesus' family.

We should also note the deeper meaning of the pilgrimage: by going up to the Temple three times a year, Israel remains, as it were, God's pilgrim people, always journeying toward its God and receiving its identity and unity increasingly from the encounter with God in the one Temple. The holy family takes its place within this great pilgrim community on its way to the Temple and to God.

On the journey home, something unexpected happens. Jesus does not travel with the others, but stays behind in Jerusalem. His parents become aware of this only at the end of the first day's journey. For them it was evidently quite normal to assume that Jesus was somewhere among the group of pilgrims. Luke uses the word *synodía*—"pilgrim community," the technical term for the traveling caravan. Given our perhaps unduly narrow image of the holy family, we find this surprising. But it illustrates very beautifully that in the holy family, freedom and obedience were combined in a healthy manner. The twelve-year-old was free to spend time with friends and children of his own age, and to remain in their company during the journey. Naturally, his parents expected to see him when evening came.

The fact that he was absent when evening came no longer has anything to do with the freedom of young people, but points to a different level, as was to become clear: it points toward the particular mission of the Son. For the parents, this was the start of days filled with fear and anxiety. According to the evangelist, it was only after three days that they found Jesus again in the Temple, where he was sitting among the teachers, listening to them and asking them questions (cf. *Lk* 2:46).

The three days may be explained in quite practical terms: Mary and Joseph had spent one day traveling north, a further day was needed in order to retrace their steps, and on the third day they eventually found Jesus. While the three days are thus a perfectly plausible chronological indication, one must nevertheless agree with René Laurentin when he detects here a silent reference to the three days between Cross and resurrection. These are days spent suffering the absence of Jesus, days of darkness, whose heaviness can be sensed in the mother's words: "Child, why have you treated us so? Behold, your father and I have been looking for you anxiously" (*Lk* 2:48). Thus an arc extends from this first Passover of Jesus to his last, the Passover of the Cross.

Jesus' divine mission bursts through the boundaries of all human criteria and repeatedly becomes, in human terms, a dark mystery. Something of the sword of sorrow of which Simeon had spoken (cf. *Lk* 2:35) becomes palpable for Mary at this hour. The closer one comes to Jesus, the more one is drawn into the mystery of his Passion.

Jesus' reply to his mother's question is astounding: How so? You were looking for me? Did you not know where a child must be? That he must be in his father's house, literally "in the things of the Father" (*Lk* 2:49)? Jesus tells his parents: I am in the very place where I belong—with the Father, in his house.

There are two principal elements to note in this reply. Mary had said: "Your father and I have been looking for you anxiously." Jesus corrects her: I *am* with my father. My father is not Joseph, but another—God himself. It is to him that I belong, and here I am with him. Could Jesus' divine sonship be presented any more clearly?

The second element is directly linked with this. Jesus uses the word "must," and he acts in accordance with what *must* be. The Son, the child, *must* be with his father. The Greek word *deî*, which Luke uses here, reappears in the Gospels whenever mention is made of Jesus' readiness to submit to God's will. He *must* suffer greatly, be rejected, be killed, and rise again, as he says to his disciples after Peter's confession (cf. *Mk* 8:31). He is already bound by the "must" at this early hour: he *must* be with the Father, and so it becomes clear that what might seem like disobedience or inappropriate freedom vis-à-vis his parents is in reality the actual expression of his filial obedience. He is in the Temple not as a rebel against his parents, but precisely as the obedient one, acting out the same obedience that leads to the Cross and the resurrection.

. . .

Saint Luke describes the reaction of Mary and Joseph to Jesus' words with two statements: "They did not understand the saying which he spoke to them," and "his mother kept all these things in her heart" (2:50, 51). Jesus' saying is on too lofty a plane for this moment in time. Even Mary's faith is a "journeying" faith, a faith that is repeatedly shrouded in darkness and has to mature by persevering through the darkness. Mary does not understand Jesus' saying, but she keeps it in her heart and allows it gradually to come to maturity there.

Again and again, Jesus' words exceed our rational powers. Again and again, they surpass our capacity to understand. The temptation to reduce them, to bend them to our own criteria, is understandable. Yet good exegesis requires of us the humility to leave intact this loftiness that so often overtaxes us, not to reduce Jesus' sayings by asking to what extent we can take him at his word. He takes us completely at our word. Believing means submitting to this loftiness and slowly growing into it.

Mary in this passage is presented quite consciously by Luke as the model believer: "Blessed is she who believed that there would be a fulfillment of what was spoken to her from the Lord," as Elizabeth had said to her (*Lk* 1:45). With the observation that appears twice in the infancy narratives—that Mary kept the words in her heart (cf. *Lk* 2:19, 51)—Luke is pointing, as we have said, to the source on which he drew for his account. At the same time Mary appears not only as the great believer, but as the image of the Church, which keeps God's word in her heart and passes it on to others.

"Then he went down with them and came to Nazareth, and was obedient to them . . . and Jesus increased in wisdom and in stature, and in favor with God and man" (*Lk* 2:51f.). After the episode highlighting Jesus' higher obedience, he returns to his normal family situation—to the lowliness of the simple life and obedience toward his earthly parents.

To the saying about Jesus' growth in wisdom and stature Luke adds a formula taken from the First Book of Samuel, which in that context was a reference to the young Samuel (cf. 2:26): he grew in favor (grace, good pleasure) with God and man. The evangelist is once again making a connection between the story of Samuel and the story of Jesus' childhood, a connection which had first appeared in the *Magnificat*, Mary's hymn of praise sung on the occasion of her encounter with Elizabeth. This joyful hymn in praise of the God who loves the "little ones" is a new version of the prayer of thanksgiving with which Hannah, Samuel's hitherto childless mother, gave thanks for the gift of her son, by which the Lord had put an end to her affliction. In the story of Jesus—so the evangelist is telling us with this citation—the story of Samuel is being repeated on a higher plane, in a definitive manner.

. . .

It is also important to note what Luke says about Jesus' growth not only in stature, but also in wisdom. On the one hand, the answer of the twelve-year-old made it clear that he knew the Father—God—intimately. Only he *knows* God, not merely through the testimony of men, but he recognizes him in himself. Jesus stands before the Father as Son, on familiar terms. He lives in his presence. He sees him. As Saint John says, Jesus is the only one who rests in the Father's heart and is therefore able to make him known (cf. *Jn* 1:18). This is what the twelve-year-old's answer makes clear: he is with the Father, he sees everything and everyone in the light of the Father.

And yet it is also true that his wisdom *grows*. As a human being, he does not live in some abstract omniscience, but he is rooted in a concrete history, a place and a time, in the different phases of human life, and this is what gives concrete shape to his knowledge. So it emerges clearly here that he thought and learned in human fashion.

It becomes quite apparent that he is true man and true God, as the Church's faith expresses it. The interplay between the two is something that we cannot ultimately define. It remains a mystery, and yet it emerges quite concretely in the short narrative about the twelve-year-old Jesus. At the same time, this story opens a door to the figure of Jesus as a whole, which is what the Gospels go on to recount.

General

Klaus Berger, *Kommentar zum Neuen Testament*, Gütersloher Verlagshaus, Gütersloh 2011.

Jean Daniélou, *The Infancy Narratives*, trans. Rosemary Sheed, Burns & Oates, London 1968.

André Feuillet, *Le Sauveur messianique et sa Mère dans les récits de l'enfance de Saint Matthieu et de Saint Luc*, Pontificia Accademia Teologica Romana, Collezione Teologica vol. 4, Libreria Editrice Vaticana 1990.

Joachim Gnilka, *Das Matthäusevangelium. Erster Teil*, Herders theologischer Kommentar zum Neuen Testament, vol. I/1, Freiburg—Basel—Vienna 1986.

René Laurentin, *The Truth of Christmas—Beyond the Myths: The Gospels of the Infancy of Christ*, trans. Michael J. Wrenn et al., St. Bede's Publications, Petersham 1986.

René Laurentin, *Structure et Théologie de Luc I–II*, Gabalda, Paris 1964.

Salvador Muñoz Iglesias, *Los Evangelios de la Infancia*, vols. II–IV, Biblioteca de Autores Cristianos, Editorial Católica, Madrid 1986–1990.

Erik Peterson, *Lukasevangelium und Synoptica*, Ausgewählte Schriften, vol. 5, Echter, Würzburg 2005.

Gianfranco Ravasi (ed.), *I Vangeli di Natale. Una visita guidata attraverso i racconti dell'infanzia di Gesù secondo Matteo e Luca*, Edizioni San Paolo, Cinisello Balsamo (MI) 1992.

Marius Reiser, *Bibelkritik und Auslegung der Heiligen Schrift. Beiträge zur Geschichte der biblischen Exegese und Hermeneutik*, Mohr Siebeck, Tübingen 2007.

Christoph Schönborn, *Weihnacht—Mythos wird Wirklichkeit. Meditationen zur Menschwerdung*, Johannes Verlag Einsiedeln, Freiburg im Breisgau 1992.

Heinz Schürmann, *Das Lukasevangelium. Erster Teil*, Herders theologischer Kommentar zum Neuen Testament, vol. III/1, Freiburg—Basel—Vienna 1969.

Alois Stöger, *Das Evangelium nach Lukas, 1. Teil.* Geistliche Schriftlesung, vol. 3/1, Patmos, Düsseldorf 1963.

Alois Stöger, *The Gospel According to Saint Luke*, trans. Benen Fahy, vol. 1, Burns & Oates, London 1969. (As this is an abridged translation, and the citations in the present book refer to passages found only in the German original, the page references relating to the German text have been retained.)

Peter Stuhlmacher, *Die Geburt des Immanuel. Die Weihnachtsgeschichten aus dem Lukas- und Matthäusevangelium*, Vandenhoeck & Ruprecht, Göttingen 2006.

Raymond Winling, *Noël et le mystère de l'incarnation*, Les éditions du Cerf, Paris 2010.

Ansgar Wucherpfennig, *Josef der Gerechte. Eine exegetische Untersuchung zu Matthäus 1–2*, Herders Biblische Studien, vol. 55, Freiburg—Basel—Vienna 2008.

Chapter II

THE ANNUNCIATION OF THE BIRTH OF JOHN THE BAPTIST AND THE ANNUNCIATION OF THE BIRTH OF JESUS

Otto Kaiser, *Isaiah 1–12: A Commentary*, 2nd edition, trans. John Bowden, SCM Press, London 1983.

Rudolf Kilian, *Jesaja 1–12*, Die Neue Echter Bibel. Kommentar zum Alten Testament mit der Einheitsübersetzung, Würzburg 1986.

Hans-Joachim Kraus, *Psalms*, 2 vols., trans. Hilton C. Oswald, Augsburg, Minneapolis 1988–89.

Hugo Rahner, *Our Lady and the Church*, trans. Sebastian Bullough, Darton Longman & Todd, London 1961.

Virgil, *Eclogues, Georgics, Aeneid: Books 1–6*, trans. H.R. Fairclough and G.P. Goold, Harvard University Press, Cambridge, Mass. 1999.

Chapter III
THE BIRTH OF JESUS IN BETHLEHEM

Marius Reiser, *Wie wahr ist die Weihnachtsgeschichte?* in: *Erbe und Auftrag* 79 (2003), 451–463.

Stefan Schreiber, *Weihnachtspolitik. Lukas 1–2 und das Goldene Zeitalter.* Studien zur Umwelt des Neuen Testaments, vol. 82, Vandenhoeck & Ruprecht, Göttingen 2009.

Chapter IV
THE WISE MEN FROM THE EAST AND THE FLIGHT INTO EGYPT

Alfons Deissler, *Zwölf Propheten. Hosea—Joël—Amos.* Die Neue Echter Bibel. Kommentar zum Alten Testament mit der Einheitsübersetzung, Würzburg 1981.

Gerhard Delling, article *"mágos,"* in: *Theological Dictionary of the New Testament*, trans. and ed. Geoffrey W. Bromiley, vol. 4, Eerdmans, Grand Rapids 1967, pp. 356–359.

Konradin Ferrari d'Occhieppo, *Der Stern von Bethlehem in astronomischer Sicht. Legende oder Tatsache?* Brunnen, Gießen 2003.

Hans-Peter Müller, article *"Bileam,"* in: *Lexikon für Theologie und Kirche*, vol. 2, col. 457.

Ernst Nellessen, *Das Kind und seine Mutter. Struktur und Verkündigung des 2. Kapitels im Matthäusevangelium*, Stuttgarter Bibelstudien, vol. 39, Katholisches Bibelwerk, Stuttgart 1969.

Rudolf Pesch, *Die matthäischen Weihnachtsgeschichten. Die Magier aus dem Osten, König Herodes und der betlehemitische Kindermord*, Bonifatius, Paderborn 2009.